Stephen V. Tracy
I. G. II^2 2336

BEITRÄGE ZUR KLASSISCHEN PHILOLOGIE

Herausgegeben von Ernst Heitsch, Reinhold Merkelbach und Clemens Zintzen

Heft 139

I. G. II^2 2336

Contributors of First Fruits for the Pythaïs

Stephen V. Tracy

1982

Verlag Anton Hain · Meisenheim am Glan

CIP-Kurztitelaufnahme der Deutschen Bibliothek

Tracy, Stephen V.:
IG II^2 2336 : contributors of first fruits for
the Pythaïs / Stephen V. Tracy. – Königstein/Ts.
: Hain, 1982.
(Beiträge zur klassischen Philologie ; H. 139)
ISBN 3-445-02231-3

NE: GT

Reproduktion, Druck und Bindung: Hain-Druck GmbH, Meisenheim/Glan
Printed in West Germany
ISBN 3-445-02231-3

FOR

STERLING DOW

PREFACE

The most important document of Athens for the years around 100 B.C. is IG II^2 2336, a list of contributors of "first fruits" for the Pythaïs. This inscription preserves a record for seven consecutive years from 103/2 to 97/6 B.C. of the principal annual officials of Athens--31 officials for each year if all had been inscribed. We possess no such extensive list for any other comparable period in the entire history of Athens. IG II^2 2336 is, thus, a uniquely valuable document. Since its discovery one hundred thirty years ago, the text has been edited four times--by Eustratiadis in 1855, by Koehler in 1883, by Kirchner in 1931, and by Dow in 1940--but the inscription as a whole has never received a full study. In fact, only the first editor supplied a commentary. I hope, therefore, that the present monograph will fill a gap by providing a rounded study of this most important inscription from late Hellenistic Athens.

I first became acquainted with the inscription during the course of research for my Ph.D. dissertation in 1966/67, work financed by a dissertation fellowship from the Woodrow Wilson Foundation. The text, commentary, and prosopographical index were constituted initially during the spring of 1971 thanks to a grant from the American Council of Learned Societies which freed me from my teaching duties. The rest of this study has been completed in the odd moments, a month here, a week or weekend there, which I've been able to snatch from the demands of University teaching over the past decade. In bringing the manuscript to completion and in revising it once again (Spring '81) in the light of a new fragment from the recent excavations in the Athenian Agora, I have been helped immeasurably by the understanding and support of Professors M.P.O. Morford and C.L. Babcock, successive Chairmen of the Department of Classics at The Ohio State University, and by Professors Arthur Adams and Diether Haenicke, successive Deans of the College of Humanities.

Over the years during which I have been engaged in this study I have benefited from the help of many institutions and persons. A complete list would be overly long and pretentious. Yet it is appropriate to say that the American School of Classical Studies in Athens and its members, the staff of the Athenian Agora Excavations, the Greek Archaeological Service, the Epigraphical Museum, its staff, and especially its two recent directors, Dr. Markellos Mitsos and Dr. D.P. Delmousou have collectively made work in Athens a particular joy. I am also sensible of an especial debt to Professor Eugene Vanderpool, Dr. Thomas Drew-Bear, Professor and Mrs. B.D. Meritt, and Professor and Mrs. Homer Thompson. My greatest debt, however, is of another order, a personal one to my two sons, Stephen Jr. and Erik, who have sacrificed most--the time which I have snatched has too often, it pains me to realize, been time taken from them.

What I owe to Professor Sterling Dow will be obvious from almost every page which follows and together they constitute the most meaningful testimonial I am able to give. Still, a word more is needed. Mr. Dow has untiringly encouraged my work on <u>IG</u> II^2 2336 at every step. He has read successive drafts, posed his usual prickly questions, lodged formidable objections (which I have not always found myself able to heed), and above all supplied unswerving enthusiasm and inspiration at moments along the way when my spirit flagged. I hope one personal anecdote will be forgiven.

Mr. Dow first came to work on IG II^2 2336 at the suggestion of his teacher, William Scott Ferguson. At a quiet dinner party in Cambridge in November of 1976, he recalled a conversation he had had with Professor Ferguson on the steps of Sever one morning before class. Mr. Ferguson expressed great delight at the new fragments which Dow had recently added to II^2 2336 and enthusiasm over the improvements in our understanding of it, and through it, of the history of Athens. Dow took especial pleasure in that conversation, he confided with a twinkle in his eye, because, unknown to Ferguson, he had with him at that very moment the page proof of the 1940 edition of *Harvard Studies* which contained Dow's new edition of IG II^2 2336. That number of *Harvard Studies* fittingly enough was dedicated to Professor Ferguson and it seems somehow particularly appropriate that this study of IG II^2 2336 should in turn be dedicated to Professor Dow.

The reader will find at a half dozen or so places *infra* sentences in quotation marks followed by [Dow]. These are verbatim extracts from notes Dow made in the late 1930's and early '40's in preparation for a full length study of the inscription. When the present monograph was in essence completed, Dow turned over these notes to me in the hope that they would be of some help in the revision. Where his notes contained materials which substantially added, I thought it best simply to quote them and mark them as Dow's; otherwise, though I was grateful to have the opportunity to consult them, I found it impossible to incorporate them in any systematic way and gave up the attempt to do so. More often than not, let me add, it was comforting to discover that our observations on particulars (made almost exactly a generation apart) coincided to a great degree.

In addition to Sterling Dow, R.S. Stroud, A.L. Boegehold, T. Drew-Bear, T.C. Loening, and J.W. Allison have read the present study at various stages and provided many helpful comments. G.L. Drummond also helped greatly by reading through the prosopographical index. Much of what is good in these pages I owe to them. Lastly, I owe a great deal of practical thanks to Cathy R. O'Neil and Christine E. Pignatiello who produced with their customary professional skill an exemplary typescript, Greek text and all. I hardly need add that I assume all responsibility for mistakes, etc.

S.V. Tracy

Columbus, Ohio

May, 1981

PUBLISHED WITH THE AID OF A GRANT FROM THE COLLEGE OF HUMANITIES AND THE GRADUATE SCHOOL OF THE OHIO STATE UNIVERSITY.

TABLE OF CONTENTS

I. The Inscription

II. Athens in 100 B.C.

III. Indices

LIST OF FIGURES

LIST OF ABBREVIATIONS

II^2	*IG* II^2.
Agora I	Inventory numbers of epigraphical fragments discovered in the American excavations of the Athenian Agora.
Agora XV	B.D. Meritt and J.S. Traill, *The Athenian Agora*, XV, *The Athenian Councillors* (Princeton, 1974).
ATC	W.S. Ferguson, *Athenian Tribal Cycles in the Hellenistic Age* (Cambridge, 1932).
DCA	P. Roussel, *Délos colonie athénienne* (Paris, 1916).
EM	Inventory numbers of epigraphical fragments housed in the Epigraphical Museum in Athens.
FD	*Fouilles de Delphes*, III, *Epigraphie* ed. G Colin et al. (Paris, 1909-1913).
ID	*Inscriptions de Délos*, fascicùle 3, ed. F Dürrbach and P. Roussel (Paris, 1935); fascicùles 4-5, ed. P. Roussel and M. Launey (Paris, 1937).
IG II^2	*Inscriptiones Graecae*, II-III, editio minor, ed. J. Kirchner (Berlin, 1913-1940).
Kerameikos III	W. Peek, *Kerameikos, Ergebnisse der Ausgrabungen*, III, *Inschriften, Ostraka, Fluchtafeln* (Berlin, 1941).
NPA	J. Sundwall, *Nachträge zur Prosopographia Attica* (Helsingfors, 1910).
PA	J. Kirchner, *Prosopographia Attica* (Berlin, 1901, 1903).
Thompson, *NSSCA*	M. Thompson, *The New Style Silver Coinage of Athens* (New York, 1961).

I. THE INSCRIPTION

HISTORY OF THE STELE[1]

During 103/2 B.C. the Athenians erected a large stele for the purpose of recording in a public place the contributions for the Pythaïs. The erection of this stele, and also, we may infer, the exaction of a fixed contribution from the officials listed on it came about as a result of the special legislation referred to in the preamble of the inscription.

> ὁ κεχειροτον[ημέν]ος ἐπὶ τὴν ἐξαποστολὴν τῆς Πυθαΐδος καὶ τὰς ἀπαρχὰς τῆς πρώτης ἐννεετηρί[δος 'Αμφικρ]άτης 'Επιστράτου Περιθοίδης ἀνέγραψ[εν] τοὺς δόντας τῶν ἀρχόντων τὰς ἀπαρχὰς [τ]ῶι 'Από[λλωνι] τῶι Πυθίωι κατὰ τὸ ψήφισμα [ὃ Ξε]νότιμος ἐγ Μυρρι[νο]ύττης εἶπεν. (II^2 2336, lines 1-4)

This legislation apparently named the officials who were to contribute and, instead of fixing a punishment for failure to do so, authorized the official charged with collecting the money to publish an annual list, which specified the title, name, and gift of each contributor. We may easily perceive how this publicity could act as a strong incentive for giving.

The stele and text would seem, therefore, to have come into being as a result of rather strong measures and under strained circumstances. The goal was to raise approximately three talents (18,000 drachmas) as the official "first fruits" for Apollo. Here it

---

[1]See also Dow's excellent accounts in Hesperia 2 (1933) pp. 427-429 and in HSCP 51 (1940) pp. 111-112.

suffices to note that the legislation was at first successful. After several years, however, events intervened and caused, apparently, a complete cessation of contributions for about two years. The list reflects this; at first well organized with the contributions of each year being inscribed all at one time, the record of the later years becomes increasingly disorganized as a result of defaults of payment, late payments, and extraordinary additional payments.

The stele itself survived, apparently intact, for nearly four centuries, lasting long enough to be broken up for use as fill in the fortification wall which was built in the aftermath of the Herulian invasion of 267 A.D. The fragments remained buried, and thus protected, until a Greek excavation under Pittakis, Kharamis, and Eustratiadis brought most of them to light in 1852.[2] Further excavation in the same area has recovered still more fragments, with the result that we now have fifty-nine in all (see the list _infra_).

Most of the fragments were found in the vicinity of the Eleusinion.[3] Some indication of where the stele stood before it was broken up, however, may come from the fact that the fragments were found along with those of 16 other stelai. And the locations of 11 of these are indicated, either generally or specifically, in the wording of their texts. All stood in the Athenian Agora and, more signifi-

---

[2] See _ʼΕπιγραφαὶ ʼΑνέκδοτοι ʼΑνακαλυφθεῖσαι καὶ ʼΕκδοθεῖσαι ὑπὸ τοῦ ʼΑρχαιολογικοῦ Συλλογοῦ_, fascicules 2 and 3 (Athens 1852, 1855).

[3] Sections Q-T 17-22 on the grid established by the Athenian Agora excavations (for the grid see R.E. Wycherley, _The Athenian Agora_ III [Princeton 1957] pl. II).

cantly, all 7 whose locations are specifically given were set up along the west side.[4] The workmen who filled in this section of the fortification wall apparently collected some of the material for the fill from the west side of the Agora. Dow has suggested,[5] therefore, that the stele stood in the precinct of Apollo Patroös. Note that for the Athenians Apollo Patroös was all but identical with Apollo Pythios,[6] the god to whom the contributions listed on the stele were made (II² 2336, line 3). However, the precinct of Apollo Patroös was rather small to accommodate many stelai and it seems entirely possible, in view of the *Fundort* and the now established fact that the Pythaïs in question is Delphian (*infra*), that the stele was set up in the shrine of Apollo Hypoakraios on the NW slope of the Acropolis. Apollo Hypoakraios appears to have been worshipped as Pythios and it may well have been from near this shrine that the Pythaïs itself set out for Delphi.[7]

---

[4]See Dow, *Hesperia* 2 (1933) p. 428 for the details.

[5]*HSCP* 51 (1940) p. 111.

[6]Demosthenes, *De Corona* 141, καλῶ...τὸν Ἀπόλλω τὸν Πύθιον, ὃς πατρῷός ἐστι τῇ πόλει...; *EM* 6001, lines 8-9 of 129/8 (*Ath. Mitt.* 66, 1941, p. 184), ...ὁ Ἀπόλλων ὁ Πύθιος ὢ̣ν̣ τ̣ο̣ῖ̣ς̣ Ἀ̣θ̣η̣ν̣α̣ίους πατρῷιος...; cf. also II² 4995, line 3.

[7]See R.E. Wycherley, "Two Athenian Shrines," *AJA* 63 (1959) pp. 68-72; J. Travlos, *Pictorial Dictionary of Ancient Athens* (New York, 1971) p. 91.

PREVIOUS EDITIONS

1855

P. Eustratiadis, "Τὰ ἐκ τῆς Στήλης τῶν Ἀπαρχῶν Τεμάχια," _Ἐπιγραφαὶ Ἀνέκδοτοι Ἀνακαλυφθεῖσαι καὶ Ἐκδοθεῖσαι ὑπὸ τοῦ Ἀρχαιολογικοῦ Συλλογοῦ_ (Athens, 1855), fascicule 3, pp. 3-60. Full and excellent edition of the major part of the stele (43 fragments[1]). In addition to a commentary containing numerous suggestions of value, the editor produced a very accurate drawing of the reconstructed stele. This edition has apparently not been consulted by any editor subsequent to Koehler; this is regrettable, for, as Koehler observed (_IG_ II 985), "In componendo restituendo illustrando titulo editor graecus ita versatus est, ut haud facile ab eo recedas."

1855-1856

K.S. Pittakis, _Ἐφημερὶς Ἀρχαιολογική_, fascicule 39 (1854) nos. 2484 (frg. _h_), 2488 (frg. _w_), 2489 (frg. _h'_), and 2493. Although dated before, this actually appeared after Eustratiadis' publication. No. 2493 gives an inaccurate text of a fragment published by Eustratiadis (frg. _o_). Of the remaining three fragments, Pittakis recognized only no. 2484 (frg. _h_) as part of "the ἀπαρχαί" inscription. The degree of accuracy of this publication is disappointingly low.

---

[1]16 fragments have been added since.

1883

IG II 985; i.e. U. Koehler, Corpus Inscriptionum Atticarum, II (Berlin, 1883), no. 985. To the 46 fragments already known, Koehler added two (frgs. b', r'). Because of its easy availability, this publication, especially the majuscule version, quickly became the standard text; it has exercised a strong influence over all subsequent editions.

1909

W.S. Ferguson, "Researches in Athenian and Delian Documents III," Klio 9 (1909) pp. 309-311. Taking cognizance of an observation by V. von Schoeffer, De Deli Insulae Rebus (Berlin, 1889) p. 244, Ferguson provided a new text of the last 56 lines, which for the first time placed fragments i-k-l in their proper position. Ferguson also made a number of interesting restorations, especially in lines 221-271 (these line numbers refer to the present edition).

1910

K. Kourouniotis, Πρακτικά 1910 p. 142 no. 8, published a majuscule text of fr. b"; Kirchner re-edited this fragment as IG II^2 2454. Dow first recognized the fragment and incorporated it into the stele.

1931

IG II^2 2336; i.e. J. Kirchner, Inscriptiones Graecae, II-III, editio minor, (Berlin, 1931), no. 2336. The readings of this edition are essentially those of Koehler as corrected and augmented by Ferguson

(Kirchner added no new fragments). This edition is notable for its wealth of prosopographical information and for the assertion that the Pythaïs in question was Delian, not Delphian.

1940

S. Dow, "The First Enneëteric Delian Pythaïs, IG II^2 2336," HSCP 51 (1940) pp. 111-124. Dow incorporated six fragments (frgs. y'-d"), eliminated the double archonship of Argeios, and attempted for the first time to estimate accurately the size of the lacunae. Dow also discerned and labelled (in the margin) the various cutters who inscribed the text.

1967

S.V. Tracy, Hesperia 36 (1967) pp. 245-248 nos. 54 (frg. e") and 55 (frg. f").

1970

S.V. Tracy, Hesperia 39 (1970) pp. 311-312 nos. 5 (frg. g") and 6 (frg. h").

1970

P. Bruneau, Recherches sur les cultes de Délos à l'époque hellénistique et à l'époque impérial, Bibl. Ec. fr. Ath. et Rome, fasc. 217 (Paris, 1970), pp. 128-137. Bruneau repeats without change Dow's 1940 edition in HSCP and Tracy's 1967 edition of frg. f" in Hesperia; he also follows Kirchner and Dow in adducing II^2 2336 as the sole evidence for a Delian Pythaïs.

1971

S.V. Tracy, _AJA_ 75 (1971) pp. 189-190 no. 7, announces the rediscovery of fragment _q_'.

1975

S.V. Tracy, _The Lettering of an Athenian Mason_, _Hesperia_ Suppl. 15 (Princeton, 1975) pp. 26-32 and plates 10-13. Tracy provides a new text and epigraphical commentary on the lines inscribed by Hand _B_, lines 48-90, 123-126, 147-149, 162-163, 178-179, 237-238, 243-244, 257, 262-263, and 270-271 in the present edition.

1982

The preliminary publication of frg. _i_" by S. Tracy will appear in _Hesperia_ 51 (1982).

LIST OF FRAGMENTS

All are incorporated into the stele (see figs. 1-4)
except as indicated in column three

Fragment	Editio Princeps	Location
a	Eustratiadis	
b (EM 5260)	"	
c	"	
d	"	
e	"	
f	"	
g	"	
h	Pittakis	
i	Eustratiadis	
k	"	
l	"	
m	"	
n	"	
o	" (=Pittakis #2493)	
p	Eustratiadis	
q	"	
r	"	
s	"	
t	"	
u	"	
v	"	

w (EM 2725)	Pittakis	
x	Eustratiadis	
y	"	
z	"	now lost (fig. 5)
a'	"	
b'	Koehler	
c'	Eustratiadis	
d'	"	
e'	"	
f'	"	
g'	"	
h'	Pittakis	
i'	Eustratiadis	
k'	"	
l'	"	
m'	"	
n'	"	now lost (fig. 6)
o'	"	
p'	"	
q' (EM 144)	"	
r'	Koehler	
s'	Eustratiadis	
t'	"	
u'	"	
v'	"	
w'	"	

x'	Eustratiadis	
y' (EM 12799)	Dow	
z' (Agora I 5734)	"	
a" (Agora I 3320)	"	
b" (Agora I 3456 = II^2 2454)	Kourouniotis	
c" (Agora I 3323)	Dow	
d" (Agora I 3321)	"	
e" (Agora I 5045)	Tracy, 1967	
f" (Agora I 5044)	"	Stoa of Attalos, Athenian Agora (fig. 9)
g" (Agora I 3318)	Tracy, 1970	Stoa of Attalos, Athenian Agora (fig. 7)
h" (Agora I 4037)	"	Stoa of Attalos, Athenian Agora (fig. 8)
i" (Agora I 7361)	Tracy, 1982	Stoa of Attalos, Athenian Agora (fig. 24)

PHYSICAL DESCRIPTION

EM 10398.

The stele is of white, doubtless Pentelic, marble. The top (flat, rough-picked), the molding, the sides (claw-chiselled), and the back (rough-picked) are all preserved at numerous places.

Height, 2.302 m.; Width at top, 0.764 m.;

Width at bottom, 0.830 m.; Thickness, 0.186 m.[1]

A number of different workmen inscribed the text at different times; the lettering of each is idiosyncratic (see the section on "The Letter-Cutters"). Variatio thus characterizes the lettering both with regard to shape and to size. The letter-height employed most often was ca. 0.008-9 m. In column I the largest letters measure ca. 0.013 m. (lines 147-149) and the smallest ca. 0.006 m. (line 103); in column II the largest letters measure ca. 0.018 m. (lines 258-259) and the smallest ca. 0.006 m. (lines 226-227). On the average the letters of column II are slightly larger than those in column I; thus, column II contains 122 lines while column I has 145 lines in approximately the

---

[1]"The proportion of thickness to width is between 1:4 and 1:4½. This is precisely normal for Athenian inscribed stelai. Normally the height of a stele was about nine or ten times the thickness, somewhat more than twice the width. To the preserved height must be added a blank space ca. 0.15 m. and a tongue, at least 0.15 m. in height, but probably 0.20 m. The total height was thus ca. 2.65 m., which is almost 14½ times the thickness. Thus whereas the normal dimensions are 1:4½:9 or 10, the present stele was 1:4½:14½." [Dow]

same vertical space.[2]

"The Lines of Breakage. In order to break up a stele, when the stone was unusually thick, or when a rectangular block of specific size was wanted, trenches were dug in the front surface. Otherwise a stele was broken up by a few blows in the middle with a heavy pick. Under the pick blows, the marble broke along natural striation lines. It is the 'habit' of Pentelic marble to break thus along straight lines. II^2 2336 was broken up by a pick (the blows must have been powerful) and the parallel sloping striations which determined the lines of breakage are evident [figs. 1-4]. Missing fragments can almost be diagrammed." [Dow]

---

[2]"Contrary to what might naturally be thought, and contrary to what facsimiles have suggested, the amount of space occupied by any individual entry has no regular relation to the importance of the official in question. Thus the important entries for Medeios (lines 182-189) and Sarapion (lines 206-214) are in some of the smallest letters of column II. What determined the size of any given letters was usually, it would seem, the letter-cutter's habit plus the demands of space. Some very large letters at the ends of both columns were intended to fill out the space." [Dow]

THE LETTER-CUTTERS

The present text, inscribed as it was over a period of seven years, reveals the work of a number of different letter-cutters. A change of hand may be taken to signify that the work was interrupted, while sameness of hand in a continuous group of lines suggests that the lines were all inscribed on the same occasion. Thus accurate identification of the hands can aid in the interpretation of the text and it is, therefore, worthwhile to establish the sequence in as much detail as the evidence will allow. As in many other respects, so in this one too, S. Dow has shown the way. In his 1940 edition he carefully identified the cutters with the labels Hand _A_, Hand _B_, etc. in the left margin. Though guided by Dow's work, I have systematically restudied the hands. There is inevitably a measure of subjectivity in sytlistic attribution,[1] but the reader will (I hope) find reassurance in the high level of agreement between Dow's attributions and those of the present writer. Where there is a divergence, it is usually because the present writer has tended to subdivide--i.e. in some cases where Dow saw the work of one man, the present writer sees evidence of two. This is probably the result of the criteria and methods used.[2]

---

[1] _Hesperia_ Suppl. 15 pp. 1-11.

[2] _Ibid_. Dow has never published a description of his method anywhere but, as I perceived from working with him extensively, his major criterion for identifying hands was the overall appearance of the lettering as well as the peculiarities of individual letters.

The cutters are labelled in the margin of the text and Dow's labels, Hands *A*-*H*, have been retained insofar as possible. A summary may be of help. In all, the work of 11 different masons (Hands *A*-*H*, *M*-*O*) can be distinguished with certainty; these 11 workmen inscribed all but 30 lines of the text. The remaining 30 lines have been assigned to 16 Hand *X*'s. Concerning the entries of Hands *A*, *B*, *C*, and *F*, the present inquiry and Dow's agree exactly. It has proved necessary to subdivide Dow's Hand *D* into Hand *D*, Hand *X*, and Hand *N*, and to distinguish *M* from Hand *E*. The entries near the bottom of column II labelled Hand *G* by Dow have been assigned to two Hand *X*'s and Hand *O*. In addition, since Dow and the present writer concur that Hand *H* made only three entries on the stele (in each case the contribution of Theobios son of Dionysios of Akharnai), it appears very probable that *H* did not inscribe the latter 2 lines of the second entry which are ascribed to him by Dow (Dow's lines 222-223). They have been assigned to Hand *X* in the present edition and are lines 220-221.

A description of the Hands and a summary of the lines inscribed by each follows.

Hand *A* (fig. 10): Very plain lettering made with thin letter strokes. Alpha (A --the crossbar is usually placed well above the horizontal mid-point of the letter), epsilon (Ε --the three horizontals taper in width at their ends until they resemble needle points), zeta (Z), sigma (Σ), xsi (Ξ), upsilon (V, Y), phi (Φ), and omega (Ω) are characteristic letters.

Hand A inscribed only the preamble (lines 1-4) and the record of the first year (lines 5-46). He made no other entries on the stele.[3] For A's role in determining the relatively narrow width of column I, see infra, p. 84.

Hand B (fig. 11): This cutter employed two types of serifs, a straight line for horizontal strokes and an inverted v which he placed at the bottom of vertical strokes. The letter-strokes tend to be thin. Epsilon (Ε), sigma (Σ), tau (Τ), and upsilon (Υ) are among B's most characteristic letters.

Hand B inscribed the second year panel (lines 48-90) and made frequent additions after that, at least one in every year except the sixth (98/7). See the margin of the text for the details. He was also the master mason who inscribed the record of the Pythaïs of 98/7 on the Athenian Treasury at Delphi.[4] Presumably, therefore, he was in Delphi during the Fall of 97 B.C. working on the Treasury; thus, he made no entry on the stele between that of the General ἐπὶ τὴν παρασκευήν of 99/8 (lines 178-179) and that of the Priest of Holy Aphrodite of 97/6 (lines 237-238).

Hand C (fig. 12): C produced letters ornamented with small serifs. His lettering has an uncertain wobbly appearance caused by two mannerisms: he curves in an awkward way strokes which are usually straight (e.g. Λ, Μ, Ν) and fails to align his letters with care

---

[3]"The letter-cutter Hand A, whose scruples have not been observed by modern editors, regularly indented not the title, but the following line, when the title-plus-name was continued on that line." [Dow]

[4]See Hesperia Suppl. 15 for a complete study of this master mason.

horizontally. In fact the letters seem to jostle up and down slightly as the eye moves over them. Characteristic letters are alpha (A), omikron (this letter tends to be very small and is usually placed in the upper part of the letter-space), sigma (Σ--the top and bottom strokes are almost, but not quite, parallel to one another), and tau (T).

C's hand appears only in the third year panel; he inscribed lines 92-122.

Hand D (fig. 13): This cutter inscribed fairly large, graceful letters with small serifs. Among his most characteristic letters are alpha (A), epsilon (E--the upper horizontal is habitually the longest, giving this letter a very idiosyncratic appearance), xsi (Ξ), sigma (Σ), and phi (Φ).

D inscribed lines 150-160 (the Herald of the Areopagos and the traditional Archons of 100/99) and 167-175 (the traditional Archons of 99/8). In addition, his hand appears near the bottom of column I in lines 142-143, where he added a late entry of the Herald to Delos of 100/99, and in column II lines 226-227 where he added two late entries, probably of Delian officials who held office in 99/8.

Hand E (fig. 14): E cut a very neat, plain alphabet. His lettering tends to be relatively small, at a maximum 0.008-9 m. in height, even when the letter-height of the surrounding entries is much greater. His most distinctive letters are A (with a curving crossbar), E, Σ, Y (with a suggestion of a serif at the bottom), and Ω.

E inscribed the record of the extraordinary contributions of Sarapion in 98/7 (lines 204-214). In addition he made seven other entries, apparently at various times and, to judge by their positions, of contributions which were late and had to be squeezed into space left blank on the stele. Hand E is identical with the master mason who inscribed the record of the Pythaïs of 106/5 on the Athenian treasury at Delphi; see in particular the shapes of alpha, epsilon, sigma, upsilon, and omega in BCH 99 (1975) pp. 202-203, figs. 7-10. It appears significant that the cutters of the records of the Pythaïds at Delphi, Hands B and E, appear more frequently on this inscription (10 and 8 times respectively), which records contributions for the Pythaïs to Delphi, than any other cutters. Whatever the exact explanation, the relationship is obvious and meaningful.

Hand F (fig. 15): This cutter's hand appears only in the entries of the Herald of the Areopagos and the traditional Archons of 97/6 (lines 245-256). His lettering, adorned with small serifs, is quite large and neat. He employed lightly incised guidelines as an aid in inscribing. Among his most characteristic letters are Ζ, Κ, Ρ, and Σ.

Hand G (fig. 16): G inscribed only several entries of officials from Delos in 97/6 (lines 228-236). He inscribed letters with serifs and tended to vary the height of his lettering, in spite of the fact that he incised guidelines. His most distinctive letters are Ε, Ν, Σ, Ω (the last being smaller than the other letters and raised up in the letter-space).

Hand *H* (fig. 17): This cutter seems to have inscribed only the three entries of Theobios son of Dionysios of Akharnai in lines 133-134, 218-219, and 241-242. It is unclear whether he inscribed the three entries at one time or on three different occasions. He inscribed rather tall, thin letters with serifs. From the small sample of his lettering which we have, Υ , Ο (small and placed in the upper part of the letter-space), Ν , Α appear to be some of his most characteristic letters. Of all the cutters who worked on this stele, *H* alone employed the alphabetic system for numerals.

Hand *M* (fig. 18): *M* inscribed only the entries of Medeios as Hoplite General (lines 164-165), as Director of the Public Bank on Delos, as Agonothetes, and as Governor of Delos (lines 182-189), all apparently at one time. He inscribed a rather neat alphabet with serifs and relatively thick letter-strokes. Α (with a broken crossbar), Ε , and Υ are characteristic letters of this cutter.[5]

Hand *N* (fig. 19): This hand presents, perhaps, the sloppiest appearance of any on the stone. The letter-strokes overlap or do not meet, serifs are used inconsistently, and the letters are crowded together. Epsilon of the shape, Ε , and an unusually large omega, Ω, characterize his lettering. *N* inscribed only the entries of

---

[5] Dow identified Hand *E* with this cutter. *E* does not employ serifs, and usually *inscribed* epsilon with *curving* top and bottom strokes, a V-shaped upsilon, and an alpha with a curving crossbar. *M* tends to make alpha with a broken crossbar, a Y-shaped upsilon, *and* epsilon with straight top and bottom strokes.

the Herald of the Areopagos and the nine traditional Archons of 98/7 (lines 190-200).

Hand O (fig. 20): This cutter inscribed lines 266-269, i.e. all but the last two on the stele. His is a very neat hand with small serifs and long, thin letter strokes. Α, Δ (raised up perceptibly from the bottom of the letter-space), and Υ are characteristic letters.

It would serve no useful purpose to describe the lettering of the 16 Hand X's because not enough letters survive to allow accurate characterization. None of the X's, so far as can be determined on the basis of our limited evidence, are identical with each other or with any of the other hands on the stele.

NOTE ON SIGLA

The Leiden System, as reformulated by Dow in <u>Conventions in Editing</u> (<u>GRBS</u> Scholarly Aids 2: Duke University, 1969) pp. 3-13, is adopted in this study, except for the treatment of erasures. In the following, double square brackets are employed to mark all erasures; they indicate a change made by the original cutter, or a contemporary, in the originally inscribed text. The matter enclosed in double square brackets represents the final state of the text, i.e. after the change.[1] Thus, for example, line 38, νή⟦.⟧σωι signifies that a single letter-space exists between eta and sigma in which a letter had been inscribed and then removed by erasure. All areas included in double square brackets are discussed in the commentary. The signs ?⟦ and ⟧? indicate that the exact point where an erasure begins or terminates is uncertain.

---

[1]See <u>Hesperia</u> Suppl. 15 pp. 123-124 for further discussion of the problems involved in editing erasures.

TEXT AND EPIGRAPHICAL COMMENTARY

Hand A 1. 'Αγαθῆ τύχη τῆς βουλῆς κ̣[αὶ το]ῦ δήμου τοῦ 'Αθηναίων· ὁ κεχειροτο<ν>[ημέν]ο̣ς ἐπὶ τὴν ἐξαποστο- NON-ΣΤΟΙ ca. 68

This commentary is primarily devoted to discussion of the readings and restorations printed in the text. An attempt has been made to credit each restoration, excepting ones which are self-evident, to the scholar who first proposed it. The prosopographical information usually included in a commentary has been placed in a separate prosopograpical index. I also discuss in this commentary certain changes of hand, especially in the case of the various Hand *X*'s, different hands in one line, correcting hands, etc.

Line 1. Dow interpreted the initial datives as nominatives. The iota adscripts which mark case are not inscribed, as occasionally happens in phrases of common occurrence (see *Hesperia* Suppl. 15 pp. 100-101); in the present instance, however, the exactly parallel wording of *FD* III 2 no. 5, which preserves the adscript of the first word, reveals that the dative case is the correct interpretation. Mu appears instead of nu. Of dotted kappa, only the top half of the vertical is visible and of dotted omikron, just a small curving segment from the upper right appears at the line of breakage.

2. ᵛλῆν τῆς Πυθαΐδος καὶ τὰς ἀπαρχὰς τῆς πρώτης

ἐν ⟦νεετη⟧? ρί[δος 'Αμφικρ]άτης 'Επιστράτου Πε-

3. ριθοίδης ἀνέγραψ[εν] τοὺς δόντας τῶν ἀρχόν ⟦των τὰς ἀπαρ⟧ χὰς

[τ]ῶι 'Από[λλωνι] τῶι Πυθίωι κα-

Line 2. Only the top of dotted omikron, the vertical of dotted tau, the first vertical of dotted pi, the apex and right slanting hasta of dotted alpha, the vertical and top of the loop of dotted rho, a small piece of the top of dotted iota, and the apex of dotted alpha are preserved. The letters in the erasure are crowded together, indicating that the mason originally omitted some letters. None of the erased letters are legible. Restoration, L. Couve (BCH 18, 1894, p. 90); the name suits the space and, in view of FD III 2 no. 13, col. II, line 20, appears inevitable.

Line 3. An erased alpha appears just to the left of the alpha of τάς. The nature of the error is unclear. Only the arc from the bottom of dotted omikron is preserved at the break. I follow Dow in underlining and dotting the final tau. Eustratiadis recorded the horizontal alone in his 1855 drawing. This stroke is no longer visible. Dow also underlined and dotted the omega of 'Απόλλωνι ; apparently this was an error, for the letter does not appear to have been read by any editor previous to Dow and the present editor can find no trace of it.

ᵛτὰ τὸ ψήφισμα [δ' Ξε]νότιμος ἐγ Μυρρι[νο]ύττης εἶπεν. *vacat* (0.309 m.)

103/2 *a*. 5. ᵛᵛᵛᵛᵛοἵδε ἀπήρξαντο ἐπὶ Θεοκλέους ἄ[ρχον]τος *vacat* (0.361 m.)

[στρα]τ[ηγ]ὸς ἐ[πὶ] τὰ ὅπλα [[ᵛ Ἀμμώνιο]]ς

[ᵛᵛ[[Δημητρίο]υ Ἀναφλύστ]]ιος ΗΗ

Line 4. Dow restored Φανότιμος; Ξενότιμος and Μενότιμος are also possible. Of the three, Xenotimos alone occurs in Attica, though not in Myrrhinoutta. Of dotted upsilon, only the tip of the right slanting stroke survives.

Line 5. Only the top left part of dotted rho appears at the edge of the break, and of dotted tau only the right half of the horizontal is preserved. This line is indented 5 letter-spaces, so that it, in fact, extends across approximately half of the width of the stele. The final letter appears over the space of the [restored] beta in line 150.

Line 6. Only the tops of dotted tau and epsilon are visible.

Lines 6-7: Hand *A* first inscribed the name of a different man. The only legible trace of this first name is a round letter (omikron, theta?) before the alpha of the *nomen*. The workman who corrected, though his general style of lettering is very like Hand *A*'s, was clearly not Hand *A*, but another cutter whom for convenience we may label Hand *X*. The shape of upsilon makes this certain: *A* inscribes upsilons which usually have the shape V, whereas the upsilons in line 7 both have the shape Y. Thus, the correction was made at a time subsequent to the inscribing of the panel. The inclusion of the

[κῆρυξ βουλῆς τ]ῆς ἐξ 'Αρ̣είου πάγου

9. v 'Η̣[_ _ _ _ _ _ _ _ _ _ _ _ _ _ _ H]

ἄρχων [θεοκλῆς _ _ _ _ _ _ _ _ _ _ H]

βασιλεὺς [_ _ _ _ _ _ _ _ _ _ _ _ H]

12. πολέμαρχ[ος _ _ _ _ _ _ _ _ _ _ _ H]

[θεσ]μοθέτ̣[αι _ _ _ _ _ _ _ _ _ _ H]

Νικ̣[ίας _ _ _ _ _ _ _ H]

---

patronymic is unusual in this column. Restoration, Dow; cf. ID 2232, lines 4-5.

Line 8. Of dotted rho, only the top half is preserved.

Line 9. Above the space between the alpha and rho of line 10 appears part of a vertical stroke; there also seems to be a trace of a central horizontal. For the principle employed in the restoration of numerals p. 101 *infra*.

Line 13. Of dotted tau, only the bottom tip of the vertical is preserved.

Line 14. Only the lower third of the vertical of dotted kappa appears at the edge of the break. Restored with a mark of interrogation, Dow; see commentary on line 15 for the evidence. Dow left space in his text after line 13 for the name of a sixth Thesmothetes. Agora I 3320 (frg. a") joins at the top of frg. g (see fig. 1), leaving no space for a separate line for the sixth Thesmothetes. If all six contributed, one was entered to the right of the title, as in lines 155 and 195.

15. ⟦Μειδ⟧ίας [_ _ _ _ _ Η]
Δωσίθεος [_ _ _ _ _ _ Η]
Διονύσιος X̣[_ _ _ _ _ Η]
18. 'Απολλώνιος [_ _ _ _ _ Η]
ναύαρχος Κηφισ[_ _ _ _ _ _ _ _ 𐅅]
στρατηγὸς ἐπὶ τ[ὴν παρασκευὴν]
21. ᵛτὴν ἐν ἄστει 'Ιάσ[ων _ _ _ _ _ 𐅅]
ἐπιμελητὴς τ[οῦ ἐμ Πειραιεῖ λιμέ]-
ᵛνος Δημέας 'Α[λαιεὺς Η]

Line 15. The initial mu is a remade nu; the epsilon is inscribed over an erased iota; an erased kappa appears before and under delta--its vertical was reused for iota in the corrected text. The mason first inscribed Νικίας, apparently by repeating the nomen just above. We may thus restore line 14 with some confidence.

Line 17. Χ[ολαργεύς], Dow. I can see no certain trace of a letter-stroke, except for what may be a slight indentation created by the end of a stroke in the bottom part of the letter-space at the break.

Line 21. Restoration, Koehler. 'Ιασίδημος and 'Ιασίμαχος also occur, albeit infrequently, in Attica and are possible.

Line 23. Restored with a mark of interrogation Roussel, DCA p. 114; cf. ID 2045 and 2255. O.W. Reinmuth, BCH 90 (1966) pp. 96-97, proposed 'Α[ζηνιεύς]; there is, however, no postively attested Azenian Demeas in ca. 100 B.C.

24. [ἐπιμελ]ητὴς [Δήλου]

[^{v}Διοσκουρίδης _ _ _ _ _ _ HH]

[ἐπιμελητὴς ἐμπορίου]

27. ^{v}I[_ _ _ _ _ _ _ _ _ _ _ HH]

γυμν[ασίαρχος εἰ]ς Δῆ[λον]

^{v}Μητρόδωρ[ος Κυ]δαθηνα[ιεὺς H]

30. ἀγορανόμοι [εἰ]ς Δῆλον

[^{v}Κιχη]σίας Σουνιεὺς [H]

Line 24. The upper third of dotted eta and dotted tau alone survives. The lacuna between lines 24 and 27 is precisely determinable because frgs. g and h (see fig. 1) join vertically at the left side (back from the inscribed surface). Only two lines have been lost. The restorations by Kirchner in lines 24 and 26 are virtually certain, for, with the sole exception of the Director of the Public Bank on Delos, they are the only officials missing from the record of this year. See also pp. 86-88 on the order of listing of the officials on the inscription.

Line 25. Restoration, Kirchner; cf. ID 1927.

Line 27. The beginning of this line is much abraded. The only certain letter-stroke which survives is the lower part of a vertical stroke located above the space between gamma and upsilon in line 28.

Line 31. Restoration, Roussel, DCA p. 183; cf. ID 2608, lines 8-9.

'Ερμοκλῆς [ca.5]ọ[– – –   H]

33. ἐπὶ τὴν φυλακὴν τῶν ἰ̣[ερ]ῶν χρη-

^{v}μάτων Θεότιμος Αἰξωνεὺς   H

Ξενοκλῆ[[ς]] 'Ραμνούσιος   H

36. ἱερεὺς 'Απόλλωνος ἐν Δή̣λωι

^{v}'Αμμώνιος <Π>αμβωτάδης   H

ἱερεὺς 'Αρτέμιδος ἐν νή[[.]]σωι

Line 32. The second omikron was read by Pittakis ('Εφ. 'Αρχ. 1854 p. 1244 no. 2484), who located it under the epsilon of the preceding line.

Line 33. Only the lower quarter of dotted iota is visible below the break.

Line 35. The initial sigma was first inscribed out of line and below the other letters (fig. 10); the mason re-inscribed it without troubling to remove his first attempt.

Line 36. Of dotted eta, only the left vertical stroke is preserved.

Line 37. A blank space was left for the pi, which was never inscribed (fig. 10).

Line 38. An erased sigma is legible *in rasura* (fig. 10).

39. v'Αγαθοκλῆς v⟦'Αγκυλῆ⟧[θ]εν H

ἱερεὺς 'Ρώμης Πυθίλαος [Σο]υνιεὺς H

ἱερεὺς 'Α⟦ν v ί v⟧ου Τίμων Σκαμ[β]ωνίδης 𐅄

42. ἱερεὺς Σαράπιδος ἐν Δή<λ>[ωι Δ]ράκων 𐅄

Line 39. Except for the numeral, this line, including the erasure and correction, was inscribed by Hand X whose use of serifs and alpha with a broken crossbar clearly differentiates him from Hand A (fig. 10). The difference in hand suggests that the name was added subsequent to A's work on the first year panel. The lettering of this Hand X appears nowhere else on the stele except, perhaps (there are too few letters for certainty), in the demotic of line 45. This entry was similar originally to that in line 46. In both cases Hand A inscribed the title and contribution but not the name, in expectation, obviously, that the contribution would be made. In such cases elsewhere on the stele, the masons simply left blank space.

Line 41. The mason originally inscribed, as Eustratiadis (p. 38) noted, AMM (fig. 10): "apparently starting to cut "Αμμωνος" [Dow].

Line 42. Delta was inscribed for lambda (fig. 10). Restoration, Eustratiadis; cf. ID 2129 and 2156.

ἱερεὺς ἁγνῆς θεοῦ Διόφ[αν]τ̣ος Μαρ⟦αθ⟧ώ⟦..⟧ Η

κῆρυξ εἰς Δῆλον Γλαυκία[ς Κρι]ωεὺς Η

45. ἱερεὺς Διὸς Κυνθίου Ζή[ν]ων [⟦Κ]ηφισιε⟧ὺς Η

Line 43. Only the right half of the horizontal of dotted tau is visible. The numeral originally was inscribed in line vertically with the other numerals (fig. 2): it was then re-oriented to the right to make room for the demotic, which was added later by a different hand. Traces of the original Η appear under ΑΘ. Two erased letters, ΝΙ, are legible after omega. Clearly they were erased in order to leave some vacant space between the demotic and the numeral. The lettering of the cutter who added the demotic is characterized by alphas with a sharply broken crossbar and omega of the shape ![omega] (fig. 10). This mason also inscribed II[2] 995 and part of the Pythaïs record of 98/7 (BCH 93, 1969, p. 372 and fig. 12).

Line 45. None of the erased letters are discernible; it is clear, however, that the erasure was made in order to include the demotic. This was accomplished by erasing the numeral and re-orienting it to the right. The demotic was added later by a different mason, as one can easily perceive from the general difference in the character of the lettering (*supra*, line 39). Originally the entries in lines 43 and 45, similar to line 42, were abbreviated for lack of space to title, *nomen*, and contribution. Demotics were added later in lines 43

ἱερεὺς Διονύσου <u>vacat</u>

<u>vacat</u>

<u>Hand B</u> 48. [οὔ]δ̣ε [ἀπέδωκαν τ]ὰς ἀπαρχὰς

<u>a</u>. 102/1 <u>a</u>. [ἐπὶ Ἐχεκράτ]ους ἄρχοντος

[σ]τρατη̣[γὸς] ἐπὶ τὰ ὅπλα

51. Σαραπίω[ν Μ]ε̣λιτεὺς ΗΗ

---

and 45 by two different masons, very probably as a result of the personal initiative of the contributors, in order to identify them more precisely.

Line 47. A blank line separates panels 1 and 2. Originally a vacant line was left before each distinct year heading, namely lines 47, 91 (see commentary), 135, and 161.

Line 48. The right slanting hasta of dotted delta alone is visible.

Line 50. Of dotted eta, only the bottom third of the left vertical remains.

Line 51. Only the topmost horizontal of dotted epsilon appears above the break.

ἄρχων Ἐχεκράτη[ς Τρινεμ]εεὺς   H

vacat

Line 52. The bottoms of the two verticals of dotted eta alone survive. Dotted epsilon is read on the basis of a serifed horizontal stroke which appears at the bottom of the lettter-space. The stroke is not perfectly horizontal; therefore, sigma is also epigraphically possible. Dotted iota (Dow) is remotely possible; the horizontal could, conceivably, be a scratch or a very elongated serif. Approximately five letters of the demotic are lost. There is no demotic ending in--σεύς; Δεκελεεύς (IX) and Τρινεμεεύς (VIII) alone suit the spatial requirements. We may eliminate the former on the principle that no two archons come from the same phyle in any given year prior to 91 B.C. (see Ferguson, ATC p. 51 and Dow, "The Lists of Athenian Archontes," Hesperia 3, 1934, p. 180), for Hippothontis (IX) is already represented by Eleusis (line 56). The Archon Ekhekrates, therefore, belonged to the deme Trinemeia and to the tribe Kekropis (VIII).

Line 53. This line was left blank for the contribution of the Basileus who, in the order of precedence observable in this inscription and in FD III 2 nos. 2 and 3, is listed immediately after the Archon. But see the commentary on line 71.

54. πολέμαρχος [[Διότιμος.]] Μαραθώνιος H

θεσμοθέται

'Αριστώνυμος 'Ελευσίνιος H

57. Θέων 'Ερχιεὺς H

Βάκχιος 'Αχαρνεὺς [H]

['Α]λκιβιάδης v Ποτάμιος [H]

60. Πανταxλῆς v Βερενικίδης H

[Θ]εόπομπος Κεφ[αλῆθ]ε[ν] H

vacat

63. vacat

[ἐπιμελητῆς Δήλου Θεόδο]τος Σουνιεὺς HH

Line 54. No legible traces of the erased text remain. The correcting hand differs from B; thus the correction is a late one. This hand is very close in style to Hand E; but, because of the small amount of evidence (only eight letters), it is impossible to identify it with certainty.

Lines 56-61. The Thesmothetai are nearly always listed in tribal order (Beloch's Law); here, however, the sequence is IX II VII IIII V VI. This lack of order was probably caused by scribal carelessness.

Lines 62-63. The order of precedence (*infra*, pp. 86 -88) suggests that these lines were left blank for the contribution of the Herald of the Areopagos, an entry which requires two lines.

Line 64. Restoration, Homolle, *BCH* 8 (1884) p. 103; cf. *ID* 1562.

65. [ἐπιμελητὴς ἐμπορίου] ἐν Δήλωι

Line 65. The two hundred drachma contribution virtually assures the restoraton, for only the Hoplite General (lines 50-51), the Epimeletes of Delos (line 64), ὁ ἐπὶ τὴν τράπεζαν τὴν ἐν Δήλωι (lines 77-78), and the ἐπιμελητὴς ἐμπορίου contribute this amount. An additional factor favoring this restoration is the order in which the officials are listed. That is to say, lines 64 and following seem to be reserved for officials of Delos, of whom the Epimeletes of the Island and the Epimeletes of Emporion are the most important and tend to be listed together (see lines 24-27, 108-111). Although no parallel for the addition of the phrase ἐν Δήλωι to this title survives, the addition makes good sense since there had been originally 10 Epimeletai of Emporion for the city (Ath. Pol. 51.4; Hesperia 43, 1974, p. 157ff., lines 21-22 of 375/4). Their duties had probably, as U. Kahrstedt (Untersuchungen zur Magistratur in Athen II [Stuttgart, 1936] pp. 50-51) claims, been cosolidated by the late second century B.C. to the one Epimeletes of the Piraeus Harbor listed in II^2 2336 (lines 22, 86, 106, 144, 220, 235). Unduly influenced by the phrase ἐν Δήλωι and insufficiently aware of the significance of the amount contributed, this writer formerly suggested, Hesperia 36, 1967, p. 246, the restoration of the Priest of Apollo on Delos.

66. [_ _ ca.16 _ _ _]ς̣ HH

[ἀγορανόμοι _ca.6]ος Μαραθώνιος

[_ _ ca.16 _ _ _]ος HH

69. [ἐπὶ τὴν φυλακὴν τῶν ἱε]ρ̣ῶν χρημά[των]

[_ _ ca.20 _ _ _ _ _ _]μ̣όκριτος 'Αχαρ[νεὺ]ς HH

[_ _ ca.20 _ _ _ _ _ _]ς Σουνιεὺς H

72. [_ _ _ ca.20 _ _ _ _ _ _]ειος H

Line 66. Directly above the first preserved letter in line 67 appears a slanting horizontal stroke which serves as the basis for dotted sigma. Epsilon is also epigraphically possible.

Line 67. A plural title is required. Since it has been established by Roussel (DCA pp. 133-135) that ἐπὶ τὰ ἱερά and ἐπὶ τὴν φυλακὴν τῶν ἱερῶν χρημάτων are variant titles used by the same officials, the only possible restoration is ἀγορανόμοι. Of dotted rho, only the bottom tip of the vertical survives.

Line 69. The upper right part of the loop of dotted rho is preserved at the edge of the break.

Line 70. Of dotted mu, an apex and the upper third of the right slanting stroke are discernible.

Lines 71-72. One of these entries must be that of the Priest of Roma. The other seemingly must be, since all of the other officials are accounted for, that of an official not otherwise attested on this inscription. This appears to be highly unlikely, for, with the exception of the extraordinary contributions made by Medeios (line

73. [γυμνασίαρχος εἰς τὸ ἐν Δήλωι γ]υμνάσιον

[_ less_than ca.22 _ _ _] H

182ff.) and Sarapion (line 205ff.), the same annual officials contributed each year. It seems probable, therefore, that the contribution of the Basileus was entered here, it being forgotten that space had been left in line 53 for his contribution. If this is so, the title βασιλεύς belongs in line 71, for the possible demotics in line 72, Ἕρμειος and Κόπρειος, belong to tribes already represented by the known archons of this year. I, therefore, tentatively restore:

71. [Βασιλεὺς _ca.11_ _]ς Σουνιεύς

72. [ἱερεὺς Ῥώμης _ca.10_]ειος

Line 74. Dow posited a lacuna, "possibly of as many as 10 lines," after this line. To judge from the other panels, however, the list of contributors for the second year is complete; i.e., no official remains unaccounted for. There are, therefore, no officials to fill a lacuna. Note further that here alone in the entire stele is the vertical distance between fragments not established with certainty. The pertinent lines in column two are 216-217.

75. [ἱερεὺς 'Απόλλωνος ἐν Δήλωι]

[_ca.7_]ι̣ων ^vv^[_ _ _ _ Η]

[ὁ ἐπὶ τὴ]ν̣ τράπεζ[αν τὴν ἐν Δήλωι]

78. Καλλί[ας] ^vv^ 'Αθμον̣[εὺς ΗΗ]

Line 75. The restoration here of the title, Priest of Apollo on Delos, rests on two factors: the position (first among the priests, i.e. he would be expected here) and the length of the title (relatively long). The combination of these factors assures the restoration.

Line 76. At the bottom right part of the letter-space before omega appears the tip of a vertical with a serif which serves as the basis of dotted iota.

Line 77. Of dotted nu, only the upper part of the right vertical is visible. Some variation in the title seems required by the spacing. Previously Tracy (Hesperia 36, 1967, p. 246) had suggested that the entry was placed on three lines. This is contrary to usual practice, except when a mason had ample space, as in lines 147-149, and the assumption of a variant title seems preferable. The title of this official is preserved elsewhere only in lines 184 and 270-271 of this inscription and in ID 1670. However, the bank also receives mention in ID 1421 Ab, lines 8-9 as ἡ τράπεζα ἡ ἐν Δήλωι , thus, the variant adopted here.

Line 78. Only the bottom of the left vertical of dotted nu survives.

ἱερεὺς Διο[νύ]σọυ Θεόδοτ[ος _ _ _ _ 𐅄]

ἱερεὺς 'Ανίọ[υ Σ]αραπίων Αἰγ̣[ιλιεὺς 𐅄]

81. ἱερεὺς 'Αρτέμ[ιδο]ς ἐν νήσ<ω>[ι]

Θεόμνηστος [Κυδα]θηναιεὺ[ς Η]

ἱερεὺς Σαράπιδος Α[ca.4]η̣ς Θορίκ[ιος 𐅄]

84. ἱερεὺς ἁγνῆς θεοῦ Θεα[ca.6] 'Α̣γ̣γ[ελῆθεν Η]

ἱερεὺς Διὸς Κυνθίου Δημήτ[ριος _ _ _ _ Η]

ἐπιμελητὴς τοῦ ἐμ Πειρα[ιεῖ λιμένος]

87. Βύτταχος ^v Λα̣μπτρ̣ε[ὺς Η]

Line 79. Of dotted omikron, only the upper part is preserved.

Line 80. The lower left side of dotted omikron alone is visible; the lower third of the vertical of dotted gamma appears below the break.

Line 81. The left horizontal of the omega was omitted.

Line 83. The tops of two vertical strokes seem to be legible in a much abraded area before the sigma of the nomen, thus the dotted eta.

Line 84. Of dotted alpha, only the tip of the apex is preserved and, of dotted gamma, only the upper third.

Line 87. The apex of dotted alpha and the vertical of dotted rho (much abraded) are visible.

στρατηγὸ<ς> ἐπὶ [τ]ὴν παρασ[κευὴ]ν τὴν ἐν ἄστει

Τιμοῦχος v Ῥαμνούσι[ος] 𐅄

90. ναύ̣αρχος Πύθων v Μελιτεὺς 𐅄

Line 88. The bottom hasta of the second sigma was never inscribed (fig. 11).

Line 89. The gouge of recent origin here and the others visible in the upper two thirds of the stele--note especially the pattern of the three large ones, two in the center and one in the upper right (fig. 2)--give evidence of the bitter street fighting in the sector of Athens around the National Museum during the civil strife following the end of World War II. At that time, the stele was set up in the courtyard outside the museum. I owe this information to Dr. Markellos Mitsos, the former director of the Epigraphical Museum.

Line 90. Of dotted upsilon, only the bottom part of the vertical is visible. Kirchner printed the numeral as H; Dow gave it as H̤ . Koehler gives (without comment) the correct reading 𐅄 , in his minuscule text; H, however, appears in his majuscule text and is undoubtedly a typographical error. This error misled both Kirchner and Dow, who depended upon the readings of Koehler's majuscule text in the case of lost fragments. Eustratiadis, apparently the only editor to actually see the fragment in question, read the numeral as 𐅄 (fig. 5) in the *Editio Princeps* of 1855.

Hand X	κῆρυξ εἰς Δῆλον Φίλων Παιανιεὺς	H
Hand C	οἵδε ἀπέδωκαν τὰς ἀπαρχὰς ἐπὶ Μηδείου	
a. 101/0 a. 93.	στρατηγὸς ἐπὶ τὰ ὅπλα 'Απο[λλό]δωρος Δ[ca.7	HH]

Line 91. This line was added at a later time in a space originally left blank between this panel and the next (fig. 11). The lettering is relatively large and nearly fills the space between the second and third year panels. The use of v-shaped serifs on horizontals and the shape of sigma, Σ, rather than ≦, distinguish this cutter from Hand B; the large size of omikron clearly reveals that these letters are not by Hand C. It is convenient to use the label Hand X and to note that this hand cannot be certainly identified with any other hand which appears on this stele.

Line 92. Only the left half of dotted pi survives at the edge of the break.

Line 93. Eustratiadis originally suggested mu; in his drawing (fig. 5), however, he recorded only the upper three quarters of a single apex. The demotic thus may have begun with delta, lambda, or mu. At most seven letters have been lost, if Eustratiadis' drawing represents the spacing and relative position of the letters accurately.

	[ἄρ]χ̣ω̣ν Μ̣ή̣δ̣[ειος Πειραιεὺς	H]
	[βασιλεὺς Ἡ]ρ̣ό̣δο̣τ̣[ο]ς Προβα[λίσιος	H]
96.	[πολέμαρχ]ος Ἀντίπατρος Κυδα[θηναιεὺς	H]
	θεσμοθέται	

Line 94. Just the tops of the dotted letters appear above the break.

Line 95. Frg. <u>b</u>', which contains parts of lines 95-99, has been badly damaged and partially effaced in the area of the present line (fig. 21). Koehler, who first edited the fragment, read δετ.ς ; Kirchner ι̣δετ̣.ς ; Dow π̣ιδ̣οτ[_]ς . The only letters which seem absolutely certain are delta and sigma, with space for three letters between them. Tau, though the right part of the horizontal hasta has been effaced, also seems nearly certain. The last five letters of the <u>nomen</u> were, therefore, almost certainly ΔΟΤΟΣ. The strokes before the delta look as follows: ι ( ) . Rho, omikron seem the most probable readings. The restoration [Ἡ]ρ̣ό̣δο̣τ̣[ο]ς was suggested by G.L. Drummond <u>per litteras</u> and seems beyond doubt.

Lines 95-96. The restoration of the titles (by Eustratiadis) are assured by the order of precedence.

	[ca.5]ος Εὐ[ω]νυμεὺς	[Η]
99.	Ἀρτεμίδωρος Βερενικίδης	[Η]
	Φυλότιμος Κικυννεὺς	[Η]
	Ἀ[[π]]ολλωνίδης Λακιάδ[η]ς	[Η]
102.	Πόπλιος Ἁλαιεὺς	Η
Hand X	κῆρυξ Ἀρεοπαγιτῶν Θεόχαρις ἐκ Κεραμέων [Η]	
Hand C	στρατηγὸς ἐπὶ τὴν παρασκευὴν	

Line 98. Only the bottom of dotted upsilon and the upper left part of dotted epsilon are visible.

Line 99. The bottom of dotted rho and part of the upper horizontal of dotted epsilon are discernible.

Line 101. Pi is superscribed on nu.

Line 103. This entry was added in a space left blank for the contribution of the sixth Thesmothetes. Except for upsilon of the shape Y and alpha with a sharply curved, nearly broken crossbar, the lettering of this line resembles Hands A and E; it can be identified with neither. The line is obviously a late entry; thus, Hand X shortened the title because only one line was available for it. Of dotted nu, only the lower third of the leading vertical is visible below the line of breakage.

105. Διονυσογένης 'Ανα[γ]υ̣ράσιος <𐅅>

ἐπιμελ<η>τὴς Πε̣[ιραιέ]ως

Κηφισόδωρος Αἰ[ξων]ε̣ὺς H

108. ἐπιμελητὴς Δή̣[λου]

Καλλίστρατ[ος ca.4]εὺς HH

ἐπιμελητὴ[ς ἐμ]πορίο[υ]

111. 'Αριστίων v[ἐ]ξ Οἴου HH

ἀγορανόμοι

Line 105. Just at the edge of the break appears a small segment of the upper right slanting stroke of dotted upsilon. 𐅅 appears on the stone.

Line 106. The initial eta has no crossbar. Only the upper left part of dotted epsilon is visible.

Line 107. Restoration, Dow; cf. Hesperia 36, 1967, pp. 88-91, lines 41-44. Kirchner read Αἰ[γι]λ[ι]εύς. There is now no trace of a lambda; indeed, the inscribed surface is gone at this point. Neither the squeezes made by Dow in ca. 1933 nor the drawings made by Eustratiadis and Koehler in the 19th century reveal any trace of it. In short, it appears that Kirchner was mistaken about the lambda. The tip of the upper horizontal of dotted epsilon is visible at the edge of the break.

Line 108. Only the initial vertical of dotted eta survives.

[_ca.4]ιος ἐκ Κερα⟦μέω⟧ν, 'Αλέξανδρος HH

114. ἐπὶ τ<ὰ> ἱερὰ

Δεινίας Παλληνεὺς H

Φιλήμων H

117. γυμνασίαρχος εἰς {ις} Δῆ[λ]ον

Διονυσόδωρος Δειρ[αδιώτη]ς H

κῆρυξ εἰς Δῆλον

120. Μύρων Λευκονοεὺς H

ἱερεὺς 'Απόλλωνος ἐν Δήλωι

Line 113. The nomen 'Εστιαῖος almost certainly should be restored, as Roussel (DCA p. 183) tentatively suggested. Traces of an erased round letter appear under mu. "The mason first wrote ΚΕΡΑΩΝ" [Dow]. Of dotted nu, only the upper part of the left vertical survives.

Line 114. The crossbar of the first alpha is missing (fig. 12).

Line 115. Only the lower third of dotted iota is visible below the break.

Line 117. Only the top of dotted omikron and the upper part of the left vertical of dotted eta are legible.

Line 118. Of dotted rho, only the bottom of the vertical is preserved.

Line 120. Just the tip of the right vertical of dotted eta appears at the edge of the break, directly under the 100 drachma sign in line 118.

		'Αντικράτης 'Επικηφίσιος	[H]
Hand B	123.	ἱερεὺς 'Αρτέμιδος [ἐ]ν νήσωι	
		[Φ]ιλοκλῆς [Κολωνῆθ]εν	H
		[ἱερ]εὺς Διο[νύσου]	
	126.	'Ασκληπιά[δης 'Αλαι]εὺς	P
Hand X		ἱερεὺς 'Ρώμης	

Line 122. Of dotted tau, only the right half of the horizontal survives.

Line 124. Eustratiadis and Koehler saw and recorded the letters now underlined. Restoration, Homolle, BCH 10 (1886) p. 31.

Line 125. Of dotted omikron, only a curving segment from the bottom left appears at the line of break.

Line 126. Restored with a mark of interrogation, Roussel, DCA p. 114 note 1. Cf. FD III 2 no. 69, lines 23 and 39. Only the serif at the bottom right of dotted alpha and the top right tip of dotted upsilon are visible.

Lines 127-130. The two entries in these lines were inscribed by two different cutters. The general impression of their lettering is quite different (fig. 17): the lettering of the first two lines is rather sloppy; the strokes are quite thick; the letters are not aligned well along the horizontal, and they vary in height. The lettering of the second two lines is neat and the individual strokes are quite thin. The mason of the first two lines made alpha with a straight crossbar, sigma with slanting top and bottom strokes, and

		Δημ<ή>τρι<ο>ς Αἰ<ξ>ω[νεὺ]ς	H
Hand X	129.	ἱερεὺς 'Ανίου Νυμφόδωρος	𐅄
		⟦^{v}ἐκ Κ ε ρ α μ έ ω ν ⟧	
Hand E		ἱερεὺς ἁγνῆς θεοῦ ἐν Δήλωι	
	132.	'Αριστόνους Πρωτάρχου Σφήττιος	[H]
Hand H		ἱερεὺς Σαράπιδος ἐν Δήλ[ωι]	
		θεόβιος Διονυσίου 'Αχ⟦αρνεὺ⟧ς	N

---

upsilon with two strokes, viz. Y ; the mason of the second two, alpha with a curved crossbar, sigma with nearly parallel top and bottom strokes, and upsilon with three strokes, Y.

Line 128. As Eustratiadis notes, ΔΗΜΜΤΡΙΗΣΑΙΣΩ appears on the stone (fig. 17).

Line 130. The entire line has been erased and re-inscribed. The second text is spaced out, filling the space of ca. 20 erased letters. The only trace of the first text is the top of the number 𐅄 below the numeral in line 129 (fig. 22). The length of the erasure suggests that the mason originally repeated the <u>nomen</u>, viz.:

ἱερεὺς 'Ανίου Νυμφόδωρος

Νυμφόδωρος ἐκ Κεραμέων 𐅄

Line 134. None of the erased letters is legible.

	135.	vacat
Hand X		οὔδε ἀπέδωκαν τὰς ἀπαρχὰς
a. 100/99 a.		ἐπὶ Θεοδοσίου ἄρχοντο[ς]
Hand E	138.	στρατηγὸς ἐπὶ τ[ὰ ὅπλα]

Lines 136-137. The Hand X of these lines is not identical for certain with any other hand on this inscription. He inscribed large neat letters (fig. 17). Consistently large omikrons reveal that he is not identical with H; broken bar alpha differentiates him from X of lines 129-130 and X of lines 127-128. Dow identified him with Hand D, the mason who inscribed the initial lines of column two. However, the letter-shapes, particularly of sigma and omega [Σ (X) compared to Σ (D); Ω (X) to Ω (D)] will not allow Dow's identification to stand. Unlikely as it at first seems, it appears that this Hand X was commissioned to enter the year heading for the fourth year by itself. Perhaps, the confusion, of which we have only the mute witness of the frequent change of hand in the latter part of the third year panel, made the demarcation provided by the fourth year heading sufficiently important for it to be inscribed all by itself. Note that the same is also true of the fifth year heading in lines 162-163; it was inscribed by Hand B apparently in isolation.

Line 137. The tops of the dotted letters alone survive.

Line 138. Restoration, Eustratiadis.

'Εστιαῖος [θε]ο̣χ̣άριδος ἐκ Κεραμέων HH

Hand X ἐπιμε̣λ̣ητὴς Δήλου

141. Σ̣αρ̣[α]πίων Μελιτεὺς HH

Hand D κῆρυξ εἰς Δῆλον

Φιλομηλείδας Κυδαθη[να]ιεὺς H

Hand X 144. ἐπιμελητὴς τοῦ ἐν Πειραιεῖ

λιμένος Διονύσιος Παλληνεὺς H

Hand E ναύαρχος Θέων Παιονίδης 𐅅

Line 139. Just a small portion of the bottom of the dotted letters is preserved. Restoration, Eustratiadis.

Lines 140-141. This hand is extremely close in style to Hand X of lines 136-137, but is to be distinguished from it because of the significant difference in the shape of upsilon (fig. 22): Y (X 136-137) versus Y (X 140-141).

Line 140. Of dotted epsilon, part of the topmost horizontal appears just above the break and, of dotted lambda, the bottom tip of the right slanting stroke.

Line 141. Only the top stroke of dotted sigma and the upper part of the vertical of dotted rho are visible.

Lines 144-145. This Hand X also cannot be identified with any other hand on the stele. For general sloppiness of lettering these lines come closest to Hand X of lines 127-128, but upsilon is uncharacteristic. Again, however, our sample of letters is too small to speak with certainty (fig. 22).

Hand B 147. ἱερεὺς Ἀπόλλων[ος] ἐν Δήλωι

Δημήτριος Δημ[ητρί]ο̣υ

Ἀ⟦ν⟧αφλύσ[τιος H]

vacat (0.028 m.)

Column II

Hand D 150. [κῆρυξ β]ουλῆς τῆς ἐξ Ἀρείου πάγου

[_ca.7_]ί̣στρατος Σφήττιος H

[ἄρ]χω[ν Θε]οδόσ[ιο]ς Λακιάδης H

153. [β]ασιλε[ὺ]ς Καλλίμ̣αχος Λευκονοεὺς H

Line 148. Only the top part of dotted omikron can be made out along the line of the break.

Line 149. Under the left hasta of nu appears a small omikron, i.e. the beginning of a phi. The mason started to commit an haplography but realized his mistake at once (see Hesperia Suppl. 15 pl. 11a).

Line 151. The dotted iota is read on the basis of a light vertical stroke which appears before sigma. It could also be part of an eta or, possibly, just a scratch. There is no Athenian name currently known which is long enough to fill the space. It seems probable, therefore, that the name was indented somewhat.

Line 153. The apex of dotted alpha and part of the lower left hasta are preserved.

	[π]ολέμα[ρ]χος Σωσιγένης Ἐλαιούσιος	H
	θεσμοθέ[ται] Τιμόθεος Κ[ηφι]σιεὺς	H
156.	Δωσίθεος [ἐ]γ Μυρρινού[τ]της	H
	Μένανδρος Παιανιεὺς	H
	Σῶσος Φλυεὺς	H
159.	Ξενοκλῆς Ῥαμνούσιος	H
	Λαφά⟦ης.⟧ Σουνιεὺς	H
	vacat	
Hand B 162.	οἵδε ἀπέδωκαν τὰς ἀπαρχὰς	

Line 154. Only the vertical of dotted gamma and the tip of the right vertical of dotted nu are visible.

Line 156. Of dotted gamma, just the right half of the horizontal survives and, of dotted tau, the lower third of the vertical.

Line 158. The tips of the top and bottom horizontals of dotted epsilon appear at the edge of the break.

Line 160. Traces of an erased sigma appear in the space between the nomen and the demotic (fig. 13). The form ΛΑΦΑΙΟΣ was probably first inscribed. The letters in erasure are cut more deeply; in addition Σ (X) instead of Σ (D) reveals that the letters in erasure were cut by a different workman and, thus, that the correction was made at a later time.

Line 162. The right tip of the horizontal of dotted tau alone remains.

a. 99/8 a. ἐπὶ Προκλέου[ς ἄ]ρχοντος

Hand M vvvv στ[ρατηγὸς] ἐπὶ τὰ ὅπλα

165. [Μήδειος Μηδείου] Πειραιεὺς HH

Line 163. Only the upper left slanting stroke of dotted upsilon is preserved. Of dotted rho, only part of the loop survives; in isolation the letter beta could also be read.

Line 164. In the space before sigma occur two marks which are apparently deliberate cuts made by the mason. One appears under the initial epsilon of line 163 and one under the iota. Both conform to the uppermost hasta of sigma and are followed by blank preserved areas equal to approximately one letter-space. It is not clear what to make of these marks. I am inclined to think that they are false starts on the title and reveal Hand M's uncertainty about the spacing, particularly the need to fill effectively the width of the column. His solution here was to indent the title four spaces. Apparently this did not satisfy him, for in the entries in line 182ff. he indented the name two spaces. The effect there proved to be a neat one which did fill the width of the column. Only the left end of the horizontal of dotted tau is visible above the break.

Line 165. Restoration, Dow; given the prominence of the man, it is certain that he held this office. The restoration, already nearly certain, seems guaranteed by the hand, viz. Hand M, who inscribed only the entries of Medeios in lines 164-165 and 182-189. These entries were apparently made at the same time.

Hand X [ναύαρχος _ca.5_ Εὐ]ωνυμεὺς 𐅄

Hand D [ἄρχων Προκλῆς ____] H

168. [βασιλεὺς __________] H

[πολέμαρχος __________] H

[θεσμοθέται __________] H

Line 166. Restoration, Eustratiadis p. 47; the fifty drachma contribution and the spacing assure the restoration. The lettering, in particular sigma and the large size of the numeral, differs from the lines immediately preceding, indicating that this is a late entry. This explains the unusual position of prominence accorded the Nauarch here; elsewhere on this inscription he never precedes the 9 traditional Archons. Sigma made with parallel top and bottom strokes differentiates this hand from those of B, D, and M. This Hand X is not, from the little evidence we have, obviously similar to any other hand preserved on the stele.

Lines 167-170. Restorations, Dow; the order discernible in the preserved panels assures them.

Lines 167-171. The assignment of these lines to Hand D is made on the basis of the observation that the entries of the 9 traditional Archons are always made by the same hand in any one year. The shape of eta congrues with D's etas above, thus providing additional support for the assignment.

	171.	[ca.6]ΣΟ[_ _ _ _ _]	Η
		[ca.3]ων ᵛΦλυεὺ[ς	Η]
		[ca.4]κράτης Χολα[ργεὺς	Η]
	174.	[ca.4]λης Θριάσιος	[Η]
		Ναυ[σί]στρατος Ἐροιά[δης	Η]
Hand E		ἐμπ[ο]ρίου ἐπιμελητὴς	
	177.	ᵛἈρχίας Διογένου Ἀνα[φλύστιος	ΗΗ]
Hand B		στρατηγὸς ἐπὶ τ[ὴν παρασκευὴν]	

Line 171. In the letter-space after omikron Dow read dotted tau. The present editor can discern no certain letter-stroke in this space.

Line 174. Only the right hasta of dotted lambda is visible; alpha, delta, or mu is therefore also possible.

Line 175. The initial vertical read as dotted nu is well preserved and unmistakable. Gamma, eta, kappa, and pi are also epigraphically possible. To the right in the area of the next two letter-spaces the stone is abraded. There are traces of what appear to be a v-shaped crossbar and the bottom of a vertical stroke; thus dotted alpha and upsilon. Pausistratos, a nomen of relatively rare occurrence in Attica, is also possible.

Line 176. The left tip of the horizontal of dotted pi and the lower half of dotted rho are discernible.

Line 178. The occurrence of the phrase ἐπὶ τὰ ὅπλα in line 164 assures the restoration made by Dow.

		Διονύσιος Δημη[τρίου Αἰξ]ων[εὺς	𐅄]
Hand E	180.	⟦κῆρυξ βουλῆς τῆς ἐξ 'Αρείο[υ πά]γο⟧υ	
		vv Ἀθηνόδωρος 'Ἀθηνο̣γένου Α̣[ἰξ]ωνεὺς	[Η]
Hand M		<ά>γωνοθέτης Π̣αναθηνα̣ί̣ων	
	183.	vv ⟦Μήδειος⟧ Μηδείο̣υ Πειραιεὺς	ΗΗ𐅄

Line 179. Restored with a mark of interrogation, Koehler.

Line 180. None of the originally inscribed letters are legible.

Line 181. The right side of dotted omikron and lower third of the left hasta of dotted alpha are preserved.

Line 182. The initial alpha lacks its crossbar. Only the left side of dotted pi, the apex of the dotted alpha, and the bottom of dotted iota are preserved.

Line 183. Along the line of break occurs part of the lower right side of dotted omikron.

Lines 183-189. The nomen in lines 183, 185, and 187, and the nomen and demotic in line 189 have been erased and, all but the demotic, re-inscribed by a different hand. Hand M employed small serifs; his letters have a neat, rather square appearance. The workman who re-inscribed did not make serifs and has a tendency to curve slightly the strokes of epsilon and sigma (fig. 18). His lettering is very close in style to Hand E but we do not have enough evidence for a certain identification. We may, however, safely conclude that the nomen was added at a time subsequent to the original

ἐπὶ τὴν δημοσίαν τράπεζαν τὴν ἐν Δήλωι

vv⟦Μήδειο[ς⟧ Μ]ηδείου Πειραιεὺς HH

186. ἀγωνοθέτ[ης Δ]ηλίων

vv⟦Μήδειος⟧ [Μηδεί̣ο]υ Πειραιεὺς HH𐅄

---

inscribing of the lines or, to put it another way, we can say that Hand M did not inscribe the lines and then, perceiving that he had got the nomen wrong, erase and inscribe the correct nomen.

A. Wilhelm, "Attische Urkunden III" SAWW 202 5 abh. (1925) p. 59ff., has given the most probable explanation of these erasures. He suggests that Medeios' leadership of the opposition to Mithridates, most clearly seen in his threefold Archonship from 91 to 88, made him a particular target of the pro-Mithridatic elements in Athens and that the obliteration of his nomen on II^{2} 2336 occurred when these elements took control of Athens in 88/7. If so, these erasures reveal a short-lived, but apparently serious, program of political reprisal against certain adherents of Rome. The re-inscribing then was done after Sulla had taken over in 86.

Line 184. The bottom of dotted iota and top of dotted eta are visible.

Line 185. A small portion from the lower left side of dotted omikron and the bottom left side of dotted sigma appear.

ἐπιμελητὴ[ς Δήλου]

189. ^{vv}⟦Μήδειος⟧ Μ̣ηδ[είου ⟦....]..... ⟧ ΗΗ

Hand N — κῆρ̣υξ βουλῆς τῆς ἐξ 'Αρε[ίου π]άγου̣

^{v}Πύρρος Πύρρ<ο>υ Λαμπ⟦τρε⟧ὺ[ς] [Η]

192. ἄρχων 'Αργεῖος 'Αργεί⟦ου Τρικορύσιο⟧ς [Η]

βασιλεὺς 'Αρχωνίδης Ναυκράτου ἐκ Κεραμέω[ν Η]

πολέμαρχος 'Α̣ριστίων Εὐδόξου Μελιτεὺς Η

195. θ̣[εσμοθ]έται 'Απο[λλ]ώνιος Νικάνδρου Κυθήρριος Η

Line 188. Restoration, Eustratiadis; cf. *ID* 1757.

Line 189. Of dotted mu, only the lower left side appears just before the break. Of the erased demotic, only the top stroke of the sigma is visible in the erased area (fig. 18).

Line 190. Only the upper halves of dotted rho and upsilon are preserved.

Line 191. The second omikron is, in fact, a theta. Rho is visible under tau and epsilon under rho, indicating that the mason originally omitted the tau.

Line 192. None of the originally inscribed letters are legible.

Line 194. Just a trace of the bottom left side of dotted alpha appears at the edge of the break.

Line 195. Of dotted theta, only the lower third is preserved.

Σκαμά[ν]δ̣ρ̣[ιος 'Ολ]υ̣μπίχου 'Αφιδναῖος H

Φιλέας 'Ε[φόρου] Πτελεάσιος H

198. Φιλίων Φ[ιλίων]ος 'Ελευσίνιος H

Βούλων Λ[εωστ]ρ̣άτου Παλληνεὺς H

Λακρατείδη[ς Σωστ]ρ̣άτου 'Ικαριεὺς H

Hand X 201. ἐπιμελητὴ[ς Δήλου]

ᵛ⟦Πολύκλειτο̲[ς]⟧? 'Αλεξάνδρου Φλυ]εὺς HH

Line 196. Just the tops of dotted delta and rho are preserved and, of dotted upsilon, only the upper right slanting stroke appears.

Line 197. Restoration, G. Colin, BCH 30 (1906) p. 183.

Line 198. Restoration, Koehler; cf. FD III 2 no. 2, line 10.

Line 199. The upper third of dotted rho is preserved. Restoration, G. Colin, BCH 30 (1906) p. 183.

Line 200. A curving stroke, i.e. the top of dotted rho, occurs along the break. Restoration, Eustratiadis p. 51; cf. FD III 2 no. 2, line 12.

Lines 201-202. There is no trace of the erased letters. Restoration, Homolle, BCH 8 (1884) p. 127; cf. ID 1619 and 1709. The hand in the erasure is the same as that of line 201; thus the correction appears to have been made at once. This mason inscribed rather large, thickly cut letters with very small serifs. His lettering is clearly different from Hand D which precedes and Hand E which follows (figs. 14 and 19).

Hand E ^v^ἐπὶ τὰ ἱερὰ Θεό[χαρις Ἑστιαίου ἐκ Κερα]μέων H

a. 98/7 a. 204. οἵδε ἀπέδωκ[αν τὰς ἀπαρχὰς ἐπὶ] Ἀργείου ἄρχοντος

^vv^στρατηγὸς [ἐπὶ τὰ ὅπλα]

[Σ]αραπίων Σαρα[πίωνος Μελιτ]εὺς HH

207. [^vv^ἀ]γωνοθέτης Ἐλ[ευσινίων]

Σαραπίων Σαραπ[ίωνος Μελιτεὺς] HH𐅄

^vv^ἀγων[οθέτ]ης Δια[σίων]

Line 203. Restoration, Eustratiadis pp. 51-52; cf. ID 1709. This line has been crowded in as a late entry.

Line 204. Of dotted khi and omikron, just a small segment from the bottom of each is preserved.

Line 205. Of dotted sigma, only a trace of the lowest stroke is discernible along the line of the break. Restoration, Eustratiadis.

Line 208. The bottom tip of the left hasta of dotted alpha appears below the break. Very small traces of the tops of dotted iota and omega are visible along the line of breakage.

Line 209. Of dotted nu, the lower third of the initial vertical alone is preserved. The basis for the reading of dotted alpha is a slanting stroke which appears at the edge of the break (fig. 14); it can only be the leading hasta of alpha, delta, lambda, or mu. Eustratiadis printed Δι[α_ _ _],Koehler δι[α_ _ _],Kirchner Δι_ _ _,Dow Διο[νυσίων ἐν Δήλωι?]. The context requires the name of a festival. Eustratiadis (p. 53) has suggested the only plausible restoration, namely Δια[σίων]. L.A. Deubner, Attische Feste (Berlin, 1932) pp.

210. Σαραπίων [Σαρα]πί[ωνος Μελιτεὺς] ΗΗ[[.]]
ᵛᵛἀγωνοθέτη[ς] Πα[ναθηναίων]
[Σαρ]απίων Σαραπ[ίωνος Μελιτεὺς ΗΗ]𐅄
213. [ᵛᵛἀγ]ωνοθέτης Δηλί[ων]
[Σαραπί]ων Σαραπί[ωνος Μελιτεὺς ΗΗ𐅄]
[ᵛᵛστρατηγὸ]ς ἐπ[ὶ τὴν παρασκευὴν]

155-158, discusses this festival; the evidence, though meager, reveals that it was still celebrated in 100 B.C. and that contests were associated with it. The present text suggests, if we may judge from the amount contributed, that the Diasia, in this epoch at least, was a lesser festival than the Eleusinia, Panathenaia, and Delia.

Line 210. Only the leading vertical of dotted nu is preserved. An erased fifty drachma sign appears after the second eta.

Line 211. In a worn area to the right of tau appear the lower parts of the two verticals of dotted eta; only the apex of dotted alpha is preserved.

Line 212. Of dotted pi, there appears only the lower part of the first vertical.

Line 213. Along the line of the break occurs a small segment of a vertical stroke which serves as the basis for reading dotted iota.

Line 215. Restoration, Dow. If the restoration in line 205 (which seems certain) is correct, then this restoration is inevitable, for the third general of this year appears in line 222.

	216.	[_ca.9_ _ _]ς Διο[_ _ _ _ _ _ _	P]
Hand X		[^v ἐπὶ τὰ ἱερὰ] Διοφά[ντος Ἀριστοκλέους Μαραθώνιος	H]
Hand H		ἱερεὺς ἁγνῆ[ς] Ἀφροδ[ίτης ἐν Δήλωι]	
	219.	Θεόβιο[ς] Διον[υ]σίου Ἀ[χαρνεὺς	P]
Hand X		[ἐπιμελ]ητ[ὴς] Πειραι[έως]	

Line 216. Attempts at restoration have little to recommend them; pace T. Sarikakis, "οἱ Ἀθηναῖοι στρατηγοὶ τῶν Ἑλληνιστικῶν χρόνων," 57 (1953) p. 291. Dow conjectured the existence of a two-line lacuna for the Priest of Apollo after this line. There appears to have been no room for a lacuna here; see the discussion of lines 74-75.

Line 217. Restoration of the title, Dow; cf. ID 1709. This line is crowded in as a late entry. The lettering is small and only partially preserved, but it is clearly different in character (Φ , A) from Hands E and H.

Line 218. Of dotted rho, only the lower half of the vertical is preserved.

Line 220. Along the line of breakage appears part of dotted iota.

Lines 220-221. Dow assigned these lines to Hand H (pp. 25, 30 supra) and they are very close in style. Not enough letters remain to enable a certain identification; however, Hand H tends to make omikron noticeably smaller than the other letters and raised up in the letter space. The omikron preserved in line 221 does not seem characteristic of H; it is too large. In addition, very faint incised

221. [ca.5]ω̣[1-2]θ̣εος Χ[_ _ _ _ _ _ Η]

---

guidelines begin at line 220 and continue through line 223. The lettering of lines 220-223 seems to be the work of the same Hand X.

Line 221. The top right part of a large circular letter appears under eta in line 220; this is the basis for reading dotted omega. The right side of a round letter, theta most probably, appears at the break before epsilon.

Following Ferguson and all previous editors, Dow restored a year rubric after this line. The recent (1967) reconstruction of the stele indicates that there was little or no space lost between lines 221 and 222 (figs. 1 and 3). Furthermore, we have evidence to suggest that no space ever existed for the restored rubric. The evidence is the relative position of the lines in the two columns. Lines 93 and 222--the positions of both are fixed absolutely by the joining configuration of the fragments which compose the lower third of the stele (fig. 4)--occur on the same horizontal line. Line 92 is placed directly above line 93 with only a minimum interlinear space intervening (fig. 3). Fragment z provides the evidence for the position of line 221. This fragment, containing the ends of lines 88-93 and the first letters of lines 218-221, is now lost; but it was recorded in drawings by both Eustratiadis and Koehler. These drawings agree in placing lines 92 and 221 on the same horizontal line. Koehler's majuscule text often misrepresents the horizontal alignment

222. [στρατηγ]ὸ̣ς ἐπὶ τὸ ναυ̣[τικὸν]

[ᵛΧαρία]ς Χαρίου Αἰθαλίδης [P]

Hand X [ἐπὶ _ 7-8 _] ἄρχοντος ἀγορανόμος εἰς Δῆλον

---

between the columns, as a result, it appears, of problems of type-setting and thus is not decisive as evidence. Eustratiadis, however, offers a true scale drawing (fig. 5), which gives the relative position of the fragments and the letters thereon with great precision. His drawing reveals that lines 92 and 221 were on the same horizontal line and thus renders it inescapable that there was no space for the restored year rubric (Dow's line 225).

Line 222. The lower right part of dotted omikron and the lower third of dotted upsilon are preserved. Concerning the hand, see lines 220-221.

Line 223. Restoration, Roussel, BCH 32 (1908) p. 367 no. 577.

Line 224. Either Argeios or Prokles may be restored. Dow restored the former; Ferguson and Kirchner, the latter.

Lines 224-225. Dow assigned these two lines to Hand E. These letters have serifs (E's lettering does not); this hand is close in style to Hand M, but, compare figs. 16 and 18, alpha with a curved crossbar (X) as opposed to alpha with a broken crossbar (M), Ω (X) against Ω (M), and Δ (X) against Δ (M) make it certain these lines are not the work of Hand M. This hand does not appear elsewhere on the stele.

225. [_ ca.9 _ _ Ξ]υπεταιῶν H

Hand D [_ ca.10 _ _ Δη]μ[ήτ]ριος Θεοδοσίου Λακιάδης H

Line 225. A small portion of the top right of dotted upsilon survives above the break.

Lines 226-227. These two lines are crowded in in very small lettering as late additions (fig. 16). Though small in size and, therefore, on first sight, not very similar to any other lettering on the stele--Dow in fact assigned these lines to Hand X--the shape of this lettering conforms in every way to that of Hand D and therefore is to be assigned to him.

Line 226. Dotted mu is read on the basis of part of a slanting stroke with a serif which appears above the omega in line 227. Restoration of the nomen, Dow. Ferguson restored (with a mark of interrogation) the title κῆρυξ εἰς Δῆλον . However, the spacing is against it. It is impossible to be certain to just which year this and the following entry belong. Crowded in, they are clearly late ones. Given their physical position on the stele, namely a little below the mid-point of the second column, they are almost certainly to be assigned either to 99/8 or 98/7; for, if they belonged to 97/6, they would appear lower on the stele. Considerations of spacing and amount contributed render the restorations ἀγορανόμος (line 226) and ἱερεὺς 'Ρώμης (line 227) most probable.

		[_ _ca.10_ _ Λ]εώσ[τρα]τος Φιλοκράτου Φυλάσιος	H
Hand G	228.	[vvἐπιμε]λητὴ[ς] Δήλου	⟦..⟧
		['Αριστίων] Σωκράτου ἐ[ξ Οἴ]ου	HH
		[vvἱερεὺ]ς 'Απόλλων[ο]ς ἐν Δήλωι	⟦.⟧
	231.	[_ ca.8_ _]νος ἐξ Οἴ[ο]υ	H

Line 227. The right tip of the horizontal of dotted tau is preserved at the edge of the break. See Hesperia 36 (1967) p. 247 for a further description of the strokes preserved here. Restoration, Tracy, Hesperia 1967.

Line 228. The erased numerals HH are discernible (fig. 16).

Line 229. The alpha is squeezed in between rho and tau, revealing that it was originally omitted. Restoration, von Schoeffer, De Deli Insulae Rebus p. 226; cf. ID 1878.

Line 230. Only the topmost stroke of dotted sigma is preserved; epsilon is epigraphically possible. An erased H is visible in rasura (fig. 16).

Line 231. The first preserved letters are part of the patronymic, for this cutter consistently included the patronymic in the other lines which he inscribed, namely lines 228-236.

[^{v}ἐπὶ τὴν φυλακὴν] τῶν [ἱε]ρων χρημάτων

[Λυσίμαχος Ἀριστείδου] Ἑ[στιαι]όθεν H

234. [Χαρίας Χαρίου] Αἰθαλίδη[ς] H

[^{vv}ἐπιμελ]ητὴς Πε[ιραιέ]ως

[[_ ca.9 _]] [_ca.7 _]ης H

Hand B 237. ἱερεὺ[ς ἁγνῆς Ἀφροδίτη]ς ἐν Δήλωι

^{vv}Γάι[ος Γαίου Ἀχαρνεὺ]ς H

Line 232. Only the loop of dotted rho is preserved.

Line 233. Under the interspace of the omega and nu of τῶν in line 232 there seems to be a horizontal stroke at the line of break. The spacing suggests that this stroke is part of epsilon rather than tau, as Tracy had earlier thought (Hesperia 36, 1967, p. 248).

Lines 233-234. Restorations, Tracy, Hesperia 1967; cf. ID 1878.

Line 235. Of dotted eta, only the top of the right vertical is visible.

Line 236. I am unable to discern Dow's dotted erased letters, Πσ_ ca.6 _ν.

Line 237. The dotted upsilon is partially preserved and very worn; only the bottom of the vertical can be made out clearly. Restoration, Ferguson.

Line 238. Restored tentatively by Eustratiadis pp. 54-55; cf. ID 2240.

Hand X   ἐπὶ Προ̣κλ[έους ἄρχοντος ἱερε]ὺ̣ς Ἀπόλλωνος

240. ἐν Δήλωι Π[ρωτ]ο̣γ̣ένη[ς Φ]ιλάδης   H

Hand H   ἱερεὺς Διὸς Κυν[θίου ἐ]ν Δήλῳ

θεόβιος Διονυσ[ίου] Ἀχαρνεὺς   N

Hand B   243. ἱερεὺς Ἀ̣ρτέμι̣[δο]ς ἐν νήσωι

Μαρσύας Μαρσύο[υ Με]λιτεὺς   [H]

Hand F   κῆρυξ βουλῆς τῆς ἐξ [Ἀρεί]ο̣υ πάγου

Lines 239-240. This lettering is close in style to Hand _G_ but the loop of the preserved rho is too large and the nu lacks the serif at the bottom of the second vertical, seemingly a regular feature of _G_'s lettering. Thus, although similar in style, it seems better to assign this lettering to yet another Hand _X_.

Line 239. The left side of dotted omikron appears to be preserved by the line of breakage. Only the right slanting stroke of dotted upsilon is visible above the break.

Line 240. The lower right part of dotted omikron and the vertical of dotted gamma are preserved. The restoration of the _nomen_, originally made by Roussel, _DCA_ p. 212, has been substantiated by Dow's join of Agora I 3321 (frg. _d_").

Line 242. On the numeral, see p. 101 n. 2.

Line 243. The apex of dotted alpha and the lower third of dotted iota alone are visible.

Line 245. Of dotted omikron, only an arc from the upper right side is preserved.

246. 'Ανδρέας 'Ανδρέου [Πειραιεὺς] Η

[ἄρ]χων 'Η[ρ]άκλειτος 'Ηρ[_ca.7_] Σφήττιος Η

βα[σιλεὺς] 'Αρίστων Π[αντακ]λέους Γαργήττιος Η

249. πολ[έμαρχ]ος 'Αντικράτ[ης Φιλίσκο]υ 'Επικηφίσιος Η

[θεσμ]οθ[έται]

Νικόνομ[ος _ca.7_ ἐκ] Κηδῶν Η

Line 246. Just a small segment from the top left of dotted upsilon survives before the break. Restoration, Koehler.

Line 247. The upper half of dotted omega, the upper third of the initial vertical of dotted eta, and the lower part of the vertical hasta of dotted rho are visible.

Line 248. The surface is badly damaged; however, part of the horizontal and first vertical of dotted pi appear. Restoration, Kirchner in PA 2155; cf. II^2 5947.

Line 249. The upper right arc of dotted omikron and the left tip of the horizontal of dotted tau are preserved. Restoration, Roussel, BCH 32 (1908) p. 311; cf. ID 2630, line 20.

Line 250. Koehler recorded the tops of the omikron and the theta in his majuscule text; these strokes are no longer visible.

Line 251. Of dotted mu, only the lower part of the leading slanting stroke survives.

252. Διογένης [ca.4 Κυδαθ]ηναιεὺς H

Δημήτριος Δ[ca.6 Παι]ονί[δη]ς H

Κλειτόμαχος [ca.7] Φλυεὺς H

255. Ζήνων 'Αρίσ[τωνος Μ]αραθώνιος H

'Αργεῖος 'Α[σκλαπίωνος 'Ατ]ηνεὺς H

Hand B στρατηγὸς ἐπὶ [τὰ ὅπλ]α Πύρρος Πύρρου Λαμπτρεὺς HH

Line 252. After the nomen Dow read dotted sigma; Koehler read delta, which served as the basis for the restoration of the patronymic as Diogenes by Kirchner (PA 3834). The spacing reveals that this restoration is incorrect. I am unable to discern any certain letter-stroke in this space. Merely the tip of the right slanting stroke of dotted upsilon appears at the edge of the break.

Line 253. Koehler read the delta. This letter-space is no longer preserved.

Line 254. The restoration [Διογνήτου], first made by Koehler and accepted by all subsequent editors, appears to have no basis. The top of the left vertical of the numeral appears directly in line with the comparable stroke in the line above.

Line 255. Only the top part of dotted rho (very worn) is preserved. Restoration, Koehler.

Line 256. Ferguson restored 'Ασκλάπωνος with a mark of interrogation; cf. Kerameikos III A 6, line 2.

Line 257. Only the bottom third of dotted iota appears below the break.

Hand X 258. ᵛστρατηγὸς ἐπὶ τὸ ναυτικὸν

'Αρχίας Διογένου [᾿Ανα]φλύστιος

Hand X ἱερεὺς ᵛΣαράπ[ιδος ἐν] Δήλωι

261. ᵛᵛᵛΕὐκ[τ]ίμε[νος Εὐδή]μου Εἰτεαῖος

Lines 258-259. Dow assigned these lines to Hand G; however, three well preserved nus appear in these lines (fig. 23). None has a serif at the bottom of the right vertical, a regular feature of G's lettering (fig. 16). Tall and elegant, this lettering is not certainly identifiable with any other on the stele.

Line 259. Of dotted upsilon, only the left slanting stroke is visible.

Lines 260-261. While similar in style to a number of the Hands labelled X and to H, so little of this lettering remains that it cannot be certainly assigned to any other hand on the stele.

Line 260. The initial vertical and a small part of the horizontal of dotted pi, the bottom of the left hasta of dotted lambda, and the upper third of dotted iota are preserved.

Line 261. Dow recorded in his text parts of iota and mu and a complete epsilon. No certain traces of letter strokes are now visible in this area (fig. 23). For the restoration, cf. *Hesperia* 17 (1948) p. 18, lines 41, 46. Note that the restoration Εὐ[κταῖος] Ε[ὐρυπτολέ]μου?, first proposed by Koehler and repeated by Ferguson, Kirchner, and Dinsmoor (*The Archons of Athens*, Cambridge, 1931, pp. 244-245), had no basis and that the entry *PA* 5772 should be expunged from the record.

Hand B στρατηγὸς [ἐπὶ τὴν πα]ρασκευὴν τὴν ἐν ἄστει

'Αγαθοκλῆς Σω[σ]ικρά[το]υ Οἰναῖος

Hand X 264. ἱερεὺς 'Ρώμης

Δημήτριος 'Ασκληπίδου 'Αλαιεὺς H

Hand O vv στρατηγὸ[ς] ἐπὶ τὸ ναυτικὸν

Line 262. Only a small part from the right side of the loop of dotted rho is preserved.

Line 263. The top of the right slanting stroke of dotted upsilon and the top of dotted omikron are visible above the break.

Lines 264-265. Dow assigned these and the next four lines to Hand G. The rho and omega in line 264 are not characteristic of G; the loop of rho is too large and the omega is large, rather than being small and raised up in the letter-space as is characteristic of G's omegas. Hand X of lines 264-265 makes alpha with a broken crossbar, which sets him apart from Hand G, and sigma Σ, which differentiates him from Hand O, Σ (lines 266-269).

Line 265. The lower left hasta of dotted lambda and the upper right of dotted upsilon are preserved.

Line 266. Though obscured by the lines of breakage and wear, the upper left part of dotted tau and the upper right part of dotted rho are discernible. Of dotted nu, only the bottom of the initial vertical is preserved.

267. ᵛ'Αρχ[ίας] 'Αρχεστράτου Κυδαθηναιεὺς ꟼ

γυμνα[σίαρ]χος εἰς τὸ ἐν Δήλωι γυμνάσιον

Δάμων ['Ικ]αριεὺς H

Hand B 270. ⟦ὁ⟧ ἐπὶ τὴν δ[η]μοσίαν τράπεζαν τὴν ⟦3½⟧

Line 267. In their respective drawings, Eustratiadis recorded ΑΡΧ, Koehler ΑΡΕ; I see ΑΡΧ (fig. 23). ΑΡΧΙΑΣ seems preferable because part of a horizontal should appear, were the letter epsilon. Eustratiadis printed 'Αρ[χίας], Koehler 'Αρ[εσίας(?)], Ferguson 'Αρ[εσίας?], Kirchner 'Αρ[εσίας]?, Dow 'Αρε[σίας]. Only the tops of dotted alpha, rho and khi appear above the break. Only the initial vertical of the numeral is preserved.

Lines 268-271. Fragment i" (fig. 24) joins here.

Line 268. Of dotted mu, only the initial slanting stroke is preserved and of dotted nu, only the lower third of the second vertical.

Line 269. Only the first vertical of dotted nu is visible. Restored with a mark of interrogation, Koehler; cf. ID 2507. The new join confirms the restoration.

Line 270. The bottom of the left hasta of dotted alpha is preserved. The erasure at the beginning of the line has no apparent explanation; the erased strokes ΕΝΔΙ are discernible at the end of the line (fig. 23 and *Hesperia* Suppl. 15 pl. 13a). The purpose of the correction was clearly to isolate the numeral to the right of the title and name.

271. [ἐν] Δ̣ήλωι Πύ̣[ρρ]ος Πύρρου Λ̣αμπρτεὺς ΗΗ

vacat (0.062 m.)

Line 271. The new fragment reveals that Koehler's tentative restoration of the *nomen* Βύττακος was incorrect. Pyrrhos, who was Herald of the Areopagos in 98/7 (*FD* III 2 no. 2, line 14) and Hoplite General in 97/6 (II^2 2336, line 257), must have held this position in an earlier year. It now seems probable that this entry (lines 270 and 271) and the entry in line 257, which is squeezed into one line and obviously late, were made at the same time to record Pyrrhos' late contributions. Only light traces of the right slanting stroke of delta remain; the upper left tip of dotted upsilon is discernible in the worn area at the edge of the break. Of dotted lambda, only the lower half of the left hasta is preserved.

THE ARRANGEMENT OF THE TEXT ON THE STELE

A. Preliminary Remarks

With the exception of the heading (lines 1-4), the text is laid out in two columns of uneven width. If one measures near the top of each column, the left hand column is ca. 0.32 m. wide and the right ca. 0.44 m. This arrangement came into being as a result of chance and lack of adequate planning on the part of the first letter-cutter, Hand A. Hand A clearly intended, at least at first, to have column I fill the left half of the stele, for he indented the year heading of the first year panel (line 5) five letter-spaces, with the result that it extends across slightly more than half of the width of the stele. In making the rest of his entries, however, Hand A did not use this width, thereby, in practice, demarcating the width of the column as less than half the width of the stele. The rest of the cutters in column I naturally followed his example.

The first three year panels (lines 5-135), even though they were not quite fully subscribed, occupy nearly the entire vertical space of the left hand column (figs. 2-4). This observable fact reveals that the original plan called for six annual panels of 30 to 31 contributors arranged in two columns, three panels to a column.

Patronymics do not regularly appear in lines 1-160 (years I-IV), probably because the cutters were not supplied with them. I infer this because it is clear from the observations just above concerning the width of column I that Hand A originally intended column I to be wider. Patronymics would have aided him greatly in filling out the column and he surely would have inscribed them, had they been supplied to him. Once, of course, the relatively narrow width of column I was established, lack of space may help to account for the absence of patronymics in the rest of that column. However, their absence in the first ten lines of column II suggests that the person who supplied the names for inscribing (Amphikrates, almost certainly) was not in the habit of including the patronymics. Note that in column I patronymics occur only in line 7 (the entry is a correction and thus the addition of the patronymic may owe to the later practice or may even have been the reason for the correction) and in lines 132, 134, 139, and 148 (all late additions, very probably not added until the practice of including them in column II was well established). Patronymics were supplied to the workmen of column II from line 177 on, in part, at least, as a practical aid in filling the rather broad width of the column. Only in lines 221, 225, 240, and 269 are patronymics absent.

As an aid in aligning the letters while inscribing, all the cutters employed guidelines, but most of them did not incise them into the surface of the stone. Incised guidelines appear in lines 131-132 (Hand E), 138-139 (Hand E), 146 (Hand E), 182-189 (Hand M), 220-223 (Hand X), 228-238 (Hands G and B), 243-256 (Hands B and F), and 264-267 (Hands X and O). No clear pattern can be discerned; only Hands F and G employ guidelines consistently. Hand E, for example, used them for his entries in column I, but not in column II; M did not use them in lines 164-165, but he did in lines 182-189; O employed them for his first two lines (266-267) but not for his second two (268-269). Whim, care with which the work was done, and the availability of tools all doubtless played their parts.

B. The Organization of Lines 1-160 (Years I-IV)

The contributions of lines 1-160 are arranged chronologically into year panels, each panel being introduced by the rubric οἵδε ἀπέδωκαν τὰς ἀπαρχὰς ἐπὶ τοῦ δεῖνα ἄρχοντος. Line 160 marks the end of the fourth panel, the last clearly defined panel on the stele. Although the officials are listed within each panel in no strict and invariable order, some general pattern of order is observable in the listing of the first four years as follows:

Officials serving in Athens:

1. Hoplite General (always first)
2. Herald of the Areopagos[1]

---

[1]The Herald of the Areopagos appears just before or just after the 9 traditional Archons. For a similar arrangement, see the records of the Pythaïs at Delphi (FD III 2 no. 3, no. 4 = BCH 99 (1975) pp. 196-197, and no. 2 = *Hesperia* Suppl. 15 p. 50). Even clearer is the evidence provided by the hands in column II of the present inscription where a notable regularity is that the 9 Archons and the Herald of the Areopagos are inscribed together as a group (lines 150-160, 190-200, and 245-256).

3. Nine traditional Archons (in fixed order)

Archon
Basileus
Polemarch
Thesmothetai (usually in tribal order)

4. Lesser officials[2]

Nauarch
General ἐπὶ τὴν παρασκευήν
Epimeletes of Piraeus Harbor

Officials serving on Delos:

1. Epimeletes of Delos

2. Epimeletes of Emporion

3. Lesser officials

Agoranomoi
οἱ ἐπὶ τὰ ἱερά[3]
Gymnasiarch
Herald[4]
Director of the Public Bank[5]

4. Delian Priests

Priest of Apollo (always first)
The priests of Artemis on the Island, Roma, Anios, and Dionysos tend to precede the priests of Sarapis, Holy Aphrodite (these two are usually juxtaposed), and Zeus Kynthios.

---

[2]These officials follow those from Delos in the listing of the second year (lines 86-90).

[3]The Agoranomoi and the officials ἐπὶ τὰ ἱερά always occur together, the Agoranomoi invariably preceding the officials ἐπὶ τὰ ἱερά.

[4]In the 1st and 2nd years the Herald appears among the priests near the end of the entire list (line 44, 91).

[5]Of the 1st four years he is listed only in year II, right after the Priest of Apollo on Delos (lines 77-78).

Officials who administer the city come first (in year I, lines 6-23), followed by those who administer Delos (lines 24-35),[6] and the priests appear last (lines 36-46).[7] The most important official in each group tends to be listed just at the head of the group. The Hoplite General, for example, is listed first among the city officials, the Epimeletes of Delos at the head of the Delian officials, and the Priest of Apollo first among the priests. Thus a partial rule of precedence is observed.[8]

The sequence of the officials in year IV (lines 138-160) apparently violates this principle of order, for the offices of Epimeletes of Delos, Herald to Delos, Epimeletes of Piraeus Harbor, Nauarch, and Priest of Apollo on Delos, all intervene between the office of Hoplite General and Herald of the Areopagos. Note, however, that these intervening offices are placed at the bottom of the first column and that each was added by a different hand (see the notation of hands in

---

[6]That geography is one of the organizational principles is made clear by the fact that the single official of Piraeus is listed last among the Athenian officials, i.e. just before the officials who serve on Delos, in years I (line 22) and III (line 106).

[7]Year II: city officials (lines 50-63), Delian officials (lines 64-74), Delian priests (lines 75-85); Year III: city officials (lines 93-107), Delian officials (lines 108-120), Delian priests (lines 121-134).

[8]Dow (_Hesperia_ Suppl. I, pp. 4, 14, 21) has demonstrated that an order of precedence is observed in the listing of prytany officials and the present writer (_Hesperia_ Suppl. 15, p. 105) has shown that such an order is also demonstrable for the listing of officials who served the corps of ephebes.

the margin of the text), indicating that these entries were late additions made in a space originally left blank at the bottom of column I. The actual order of inscribing may well have been Hoplite General, Herald of the Areopagos, and nine traditional Archons, in complete conformity with the order observable in the first three panels.

C. The Year Headings

All previous editors of this inscription have restored either eight or seven year headings, creating seven or eight regular year panels. The most recent editor, Dow, following Ferguson, restored after line 221 as a year rubric for the seventh year (97/6), οἵδε ἀπέδωκαν τὰς ἀπαρχὰς ἐπὶ Ἡρακλείτου. We have already ascertained (epigraphical commentary *ad loc.*) that no space existed at this point for the heading.[9] Where was the seventh year rubric inscribed then, if not here? There is no room for it at any other place on the stele and the conclusion can only be that it never existed.

This is not so drastic a conclusion as it may seem, especially when one perceives the increasingly random and confused way in which entries were made in the list. The panels of the first (103/2) and the second

---

[9]Even if there were space, it would be difficult to imagine that it was placed here, for the official listed just after this point, lines 222-223, held office in 98/7 and not 97/6 (p. 122 *infra* and the prosopographical index on Kharias of Aithalidai).

year (102/1) are the most complete and regular. Each was inscribed almost *in toto* by one mason, a different one for each year.[10] Obviously accounts were kept and payments received in such a way that the record could be inscribed all at once, probably at or near the end of the year. In the record of the third year (101/0), this regular practice had already begun to break down: all of the secular government officials plus one priest appear first (lines 93-122), inscribed by Hand *C*; then six further entries, all contributions of priests, follow (lines 123-134); these were inscribed by five different cutters, *scil*. at five different times, subsequent to the inscribing of the principal group of officials. Evidently there had been some change.

In the record of the fourth year (100/99) and after, the high frequency of change of cutter continued. The majority of these entries were thus made at different times and this in turn presupposes an irregular system for collecting and recording the contributions. The drop in the number of contributors from 27 in the third to 16 in the fourth year is notable (p. 102 *infra*) and graphically reveals that difficulties were encountered in collecting the contributions for that year.

In spite of the high frequency of the change of workman and the fluctuation in number of contributors, one regularity is, however, observable throughout the record: the Hoplite General, the Herald of the Areopagos, and the nine traditional Archons are usually grouped to-

---

[10]See the section on "The Letter-Cutters," the notation of hands in the margin of the text, and the epigraphical commentary for the evidence documenting the hands throughout this discussion.

gether in the record of any one year and are often inscribed by one cutter. Part of their official obligations, it seems, included a contribution for the Pythaïs. Their donations were probably made at one time, as if by agreement, and thus could be inscribed all together. Since they are among the most important Athenian officials and since they represent a constant in the text, their relative position in the record of each year should be revealing.

In years I-V they are listed first, as one might expect, directly after the heading.[11] The heading in each of these years therefore clearly marks the beginning of the record for that year. In year VI (98/7) this logical arrangement, which consists of (1) heading, (2) most important city officials, disappears. The heading appears instead in line 204 after the Herald of the Areopagos and the nine Archons (who are entered in lines 190-200). The Herald of the Areopagos and the Archons of 98/7 are thus listed technically under 99/8 and are followed by two officials (in lines 201-203) who are known to have held office in 99/8.

Leaving aside the question of what happened, let us determine, if we can, when it happened. The key to this lies in the pattern of occurrence of the hands. The year headings for 100/99 (lines 136-137) and 99/8 (lines 162-163) are anomalous.[12] That is to say, normally a cutter inscribed the year heading and a group of officials under it.

---

[11]On the apparent anomalies in years IV and V, *supra*, pp. 88-89 and 63 respectively.

[12]See the epigraphical commentary on lines 136-137.

These two headings alone are exceptional, for in each case the cutter (a different one for each heading) inscribed only the heading, presumably because no contributions had yet come in to be entered or, only a few, from the minor officials. Thus at the end of the year 100/99 and also of 99/8 few or no contributions had been made by the leading officials of the State. At the close of each year, however, in order to preserve the order by year panels and in expectation that contributions would be made, someone, presumably Amphikrates of Perithoidai (II^2 2336_2) or a subordinate, hired a mason to inscribe the year heading on the stele and to approximate its proper position, thus delineating the major parts of the text and providing a guide for the workmen who would be faced with inscribing the expected late entries. Sequentially speaking, the next significant group of entries on the stele was made by Hand D who, leaving some spaces blank in the records of both years for officials whose contributions were expected but had not yet been received, inscribed late in 99/8, or perhaps even sometime in 98/7, the contributions of the traditional Archons both of 100/99 (lines 150-160) and 99/8 (lines 167-175). That he was commissioned to inscribe both groups at the same time is also suggested by the fact that patronymics are absent from both groups. Masons who inscribed later were regularly provided with the patronymics (*supra*, p. 85). In sum the evidence suggests a drastic curtailment, probably a total cessation, of payments from late 100/99 to late 99/8 or early 98/7, when Hand D made his entries.

There then followed, it seems clear, in rapid chronological succession the extraordinary contributions of Medeios (lines 164-165, 182-189), those of the Archons of 98/7 (190-200), and the extraordinary contributions of Sarapion (lines 204-214). These contributions form a related group, for they all were made during 98/7. Medeios' entries in lines 165 and 182-189 were inscribed by a single workman and thus all at one time. Last among the offices listed appears his Governorship of Delos (line 189) which he held in 98/7; therefore, these entries cannot have been made until sometime in 98/7. At about this same time, both the Archons of 98/7 and Sarapion of Melite made their contributions. Note that Sarapion's entries are immediately preceded by the year-heading for that year (line 204), which in fact is used to date them. The contributions recorded in lines 182-214 thus form a group which were made rather close together in time, in an obvious attempt to make up for the low rate of subscription in the fourth and initial phase of the fifth year. It is no doubt more than coincidence that this significant effort to collect revenue came in the year 98/7, the year when the Pythaïs went to Delphi, and that the person who contributed most, Sarapion of Melite, was both Hoplite General and leader of the Pythaïs in 98/7.[13] It seems clear that after the long interruption in giving in the fourth and fifth years (100/99-99/8), the list in essence changed character from an annual record of annual contributions to a somewhat disorganized record of a last-minute fund-raising effort to support the Pythaïs scheduled to go to Delphi at the close of the year 98/7.

---

[13] _FD_ III 2 no. 6, lines 2-7 = _Hesperia_ Suppl. 15 p. 48.

To return to the year headings--Medeios' extraordinary contributions (lines 164-165, 182-189) mark the first real departure in the use of the year heading. Although listed under 99/8, he made them in 98/7 and gave in several different capacities, i.e. as Hoplite General, Director of the Public Bank on Delos, and as Epimeletes of the Island, offices held in 99/8, 100/99,[14] and 98/7. Here for the first time in the list there existed, necessarily, a clear discrepancy between the time when an official held office and the time when he made his contribution. By this time, therefore, the year heading which indicated the simultaneity of both had lost its full meaning. Sarapion then followed by employing the formal year heading, οἵδε ἀπέδωκαν κτλ., to introduce and date the record of his extraordinary liturgies (lines 204-214), but it is in reality simply a marker for his contributions and not a bona fide year heading.[15] In a real sense there exists no functional year heading, dating both the office and the contribution of each official listed under it, after lines 136-137.

---

[14]The date of his incumbency as Director of the Public Bank most probably belongs to this year. The years 101/0, 99/8 and 98/7 may be eliminated since it is impossible that he held this office simultaneously with another annual office. Kallias of Athmonon held the post in 102/1. Of the remaining years, 97/6 is impossible because these entries were made in 98/7 and 103/2 unlikely because in that year Medeios had not yet held one of the Nine Archonships and thus been admitted to the Areopagos.

[15]Note that the traditional Archons of 98/7 had already been listed (lines 190-200) and that an entry following is that of an official who held office in 99/8 (line 217).

When, then, were the contributions of the officials of 97/6 made and why were they not introduced by a year heading? The internal evidence of the text, as we have seen, reveals that the contributions of II^2 2336 were connected with the dispatch of the Pythaïs to Delphi at the end of the year 98/7. It is logical, therefore, to suppose that the last planned, official subscription year on II^2 2336 was 98/7, the sixth year, and that the contributions from officials of 97/6 were looked upon as supplemental to a collection period which officially terminated in 98/7.[16] We may conclude that this is the reason why the officials of 97/6 are not accorded a year heading on the inscription.

The Pythaïs went to Delphi at the close of the year 98/7 as scheduled. It is doubtful whether many of the officials of 97/6 can have contributed before its departure, for they would not even have entered upon their year in office until after the Pythaïs had taken place. It is a priori probable, therefore, that all or most of their contributions (listed on the stele in line 228ff.) were made after the Pythaïs had gone to Delphi and returned to Athens. The frequent appearance of Hand _B_ (5 times) in this part of the list lends support to this view. Hand _B_ inscribed the record of the Pythaïs of 98/7 on the south wall of the Athenian treasury at Delphi. Thus he was in Delphi at the end of the year 98/7 and the beginning of 97/6. He can, therefore, have only made these entries on II^2 2336 after he returned from Delphi (see p. 27).

---

[16]The spacing of the list also strongly suggests that a six-year collection was planned; _supra_, p. 84.

It becomes apparent that at the time when the Pythaïs went to Delphi something less than the total funds recorded on II^2 2336 had actually been collected. Furthermore, the fact that the collection and recording of contributions continued after the Pythaïs suggests that the Athenians had committed themselves to raising a certain amount of money (3 talents, 18,000 drachmas, probably) as "first fruits" from the State for Pythian Apollo. Perhaps the contributions of the officials of 97/6 were dispatched to Delphi at the end of 97/6 to fulfill the obligation or were used to reimburse another source which had provided money on a temporary basis to make up the shortfall. In any case, some pressure evidently existed to raise a fixed sum of money as ἀπαρχαί for Pythian Apollo.

In summary, the inscribed text yields up evidence of three overlapping, but fairly distinct, stages in the raising of the funds recorded on II^2 2336. The list came into being in 103/2, was planned originally as an annual record of annual contributions, and was scheduled to continue for six years. The intention was to raise as ἀπαρχαί approximately 1/2 talent (3,000 drachmas) per year. For the first three years (lines 1-134) things went about as planned, with all of the contributions of a given year being inscribed by one hand, scil. at one time, probably at the close of the year. However, already in the third year there are signs of trouble; the contributions of the Delian priests (lines 123-134) apparently came in late and not all at once, since they were inscribed by five different hands and not by the workman who inscribed the main block of contributions for that year.

There then occurred a complete break in the record[17] and, thus, in the contributions for about two years (100/99-99/8) followed by a last-minute extraordinary fund-raising effort in 98/7 (lines 135-ca. 214). Sarapion and Medeios led this effort, which, however, still fell short of the projected goal. The final stage was a supplemental set of contributions solicited from officials of 97/6 and from officials of earlier years who had not yet paid (lines 215-271).

D. Appendix:

The Dates of the Officials in Lines 182-271

As the preceding has revealed, the year heading cannot be accepted as a reliable guide for the date of an official's incumbency in office from line 182 to the bottom of the stele. In the following list, the evidence for the date of each official in these lines is given. Where independent evidence is lacking, the following principles have guided the assignment of date. Entries inscribed together by the same hand are considered to belong to the same year; entries are presumed to belong to the same year as those which precede and follow. A question mark should be interpreted as a warning that no independent evidence exists for the assigned date other than a general probability arising from the relative position of the entry on the stele.

Line	Year	Citations, Evidence
182-183	99/8	This Agonothesia was probably fulfilled by the Hoplite General
184-185	100/99	*Supra*, p. 94 n. 14

---

[17]This break was probably caused by the slave revolt of about 100 B.C. On this see *HSCP* 83 (1979) pp. 232-234.

186-187	98/7	Perhaps he exercised this Agonothesia when he was Epimeletes of the Island.
188-189	98/7	ID 1757 and ID 1711.
190-200	98/7	FD III 2 nos. 10 and 2, lines 15-26 = Hesperia Suppl. 15 p. 50.
201-202	99/8	ID 1619 and 1709.
203	99/8	ID 1709, line 10.
204-206	98/7	
207-208	98/7	There is some evidence to suggest that the Hoplite General played an important role in this festival,[18] perhaps as Agonothetes(?).
209-210	ca. 98/7	
211-212	102/1 or 98/7	The Hoplite General probably performed this Agonothesia during his year in office.
213-214	100/99	This Agonothesia probably dates to his term as Epimeletes of Delos.
215-216	98/7	P. 124 *infra*.
217	99/8	ID 1709, line 9.
218-219	99/8?	P. 140 *infra*.
220-221	99/8?	P. 121 *infra*.
222-223	98/7	The relative position of the entry plus the fact that he was ἐπὶ τὰ ἱερά in 97/6 and mint magistrate most probably in 99/8 (see prosopographical index) make this date certain. See also p. 122 *infra*.
224-225	99/8?	See epigraphical commentary.
226	99/8?	See epigraphical commentary.
227	99/8?	See epigraphical commentary.

[18] D.J. Geagan, *The Athenian Constitution after Sulla*, *Hesperia* Suppl. 12 (Princeton, 1967) pp. 23-24.

228-229	97/6	*ID* 1878.
230-231	97/6	The same cutter inscribed the entries in lines 228-236.
232-234	97/6	*ID* 1878.
235-236	97/6	
237-238	97/6?	P. 140 *infra*.
239-240	99/8	
241-242	97/6	*ID* 1878, 1892.
243-244	97/6	Tribal rotation assures the date (p. 137 *infra*).
245-256	97/6	These are the traditional Archons of the year 97/6.
257	97/6	The position on the stele and process of elimination assure the date.
258-259	101/0 or 97/6	It seems more probable that he was General ἐπὶ τὸ ναυτικόν *before* serving as Epimeletes of Emporion (99/8) rather than after.
260-261	97/6	Tribal rotation assures the date (p. 139 *infra*).
262-263	100/99 or 97/6	P. 124 *infra*.
264-265	97/6?	
266-267	97/6 or 101/0	See the comment immediately above on lines 258-259.
268-269	97/6?	
270-271	99/8	He was Herald of the Areopagos in 98/7 and Hoplite General in 97/6. He could also have held this position in 103/2 or 101/0.

THE CONTRIBUTIONS

Checklist of Contributing Officials and Amount Contributed (Years I-IV)

Title	Year I (103/2)	Year II (102/1)	Year III (101/0)	Year IV (100/99)	Amount
Hoplite General	X	X	X	X	200
Herald of the Areopagos	X	0	X	X	100
Archon	X	X	X	X	100
Basileus	X	(X?)	[X]	X	100
Polemarch	X	X	X	X	100
Thesmothetes	[X]	X	X	X	100
Thesmothetes	X	X	X	X	100
Thesmothetes	X	X	X	X	100
Thesmothetes	X	X	X	X	100
Thesmothetes	X	X	X	X	100
Thesmothetes	X	X	0	X	100
Nauarch	X	X	0[1]	X	50
General ἐπὶ τὴν παρασκευήν	X	X	X	0	50
Epimeletes of Piraeus Harbor	X	X	X	X	100
Epimeletes of Delos	[X]	[X]	X	X	200
Epimeletes of Emporion	[X]	[X]	X	0	200
Gymnasiarch on Delos	X	X	X	0	100
Agoranomos on Delos	X	[X]	X	0	100
Agoranomos on Delos	X	[X]	X	0	100
ἐπὶ τὰ ἱερά	X	X	X	0	100
ἐπὶ τὰ ἱερά	X	X	X	0	100
Priest of Apollo on Delos	X	[X]	X	X	100
Priest of Artemis on the Island	X	X	X	0	100
Priest of Roma	X	(X?)	X	0	100
Priest of Anios	X	X	X	0	50
Priest of Sarapis on Delos	X	X	X	0	50

[1]He made a very late contribution which is recorded in lines 258-259. It is not counted here because the present list attempts to give the state of affairs at the time regular contributions were being made for a given year. This is also true for the Director of the Public Bank on Delos in 100/99 who did not contribute until 98/7 (lines 184-185).

Priest of ἁγνῆς Ἀφροδίτης	X	X	X	0	100
Herald to Delos	X	X	X	X	100
Priest of Zeus Kynthios	X	X	0	0	100
Priest of Dionysos	X	X	X	0	50
Director of the Public Bank on Delos	0	X	0	0	200
Total Number of Contributors	30	30	27	16	103
Total Amount Contributed	3050 Dr.	3150 Dr.	2800 Dr.	1750 Dr.	10,750 Dr.

X = preserved
[X] = restored--restoration certain
(X?) = not preserved or restored but probably contributed
0 = did not contribute

With one possible exception, a given official contributes the same amount each time.[2] The amounts were fixed at 50, 100 or 200 drachmas. The Hoplite General in every preserved instance gives 200 drachmas, the Archon 100, the General ἐπὶ τὴν παρασκευήν 50, etc. The restoration of numerals in the text has been made on the basis of this observation. Twenty-two of the thirty-one officials contributed 100 drachmas and that was clearly the regular amount. The Hoplite General, the Epimeletes of Delos, the Epimeletes of Emporion, and the Director of the Public Bank pay 200; the Nauarch, the General ἐπὶ τὴν παρασκευήν , and the Priests of Anios, Sarapis, and Dionysos contribute 50. In general a greater or lesser amount marks more important and less important offices.

---

[2]The priest of Zeus Kynthios is recorded as having contributed 50 instead of 100 drachmas in line 242. This is very probably a mistake by the mason (Hand H) who employed the alphabetic system for all his entries; he probably misread acrophonic H (100) as N (50), for he inscribed N.

The drop in the number of contributions to 16 in the fourth year (100/99) is startling. Only about half of the officials of this year ever contributed. And even the most important officials experienced difficulties in contributing on time. Note that the contributions of the Hoplite General (lines 138-139), the Epimeletes of the Island (lines 140-141), the Director of the Public Bank (lines 184-185), and the Priest of Apollo (lines 147-149) are all clearly late payments. Furthermore, 14 officials of this year never contributed at all, primarily those who served on Delos.[3]

Ferguson supposed that the Delian officials objected to contributing for a festival in which they could not hope to participate.[4] If this were an operative factor, nearly all of the contributors shared it, for participation in the Pythaïs was _ex officio_ and was limited to the Archons of 98/7. Indeed, of the 121 individuals identifiable on II^2 2336, only 14 actually participated in the Pythaïs of 98/7 and four others had close relatives who were participants. In addition to the Hoplite General, the Herald of the Areopagos, and the nine traditional Archons of 98/7, Amphikrates of Perithoidai, Glaukias of Krioa, and Herodotos of Probalinthos took part. Ammonios of Anaphlystos, Buttakos of Lamptrai, Polykleitos of Phlya, and Timouchos of Rhamnous had relatives who participated (see the prosopographical index for details).

---

[3]Another, and probably more accurate, way to look at it is that the minor officials could not reasonably be pressured much after the fact to contribute and so most of them did not, except for the nine Archons who had special traditional status and gave as a group. The only major official of 100/99 who failed to make his payment was the Epimeletes of Emporion.

[4]"Researches III," _Klio_ 9 (1909) p. 314.

We are now in a position to know that the cause was something more serious than the petty jealousies between rival cities or shrines which Ferguson's remarks imply. It is clear from our discussion of the year headings above that the disruption was a major one which not only hindered the participation of the officials of 100/99 but totally disrupted the process for about two years.

Checklist of Contributing Officials and Amounts Contributed
(Years V-VII)

Title	Year V (99/8)	Year VI (98/7)	Supplemental Contributions of Officials of 97/6	Amount
Hoplite General	X	X	X	200
Herald of the Areopagos	X	X	X	100
Archon	[X]	X	X	100
Basileus	[X]	X	X	100
Polemarch	[X]	X	X	100
Thesmothetes	[X]	X	X	100
Thesmothetes	X	X	X	100
Thesmothetes	X	X	X	100
Thesmothetes	X	X	X	100
Thesmothetes	X	X	X	100
Thesmothetes	X	X	X	100
Nauarch	[X]	X	X	50
General ἐπὶ τὴν παρασκευήν	X	[X]	X	50
Epimeletes of Piraeus Harbor	X	0	X	100
Epimeletes of Delos	X	X	X	200
Epimeletes of Emporion	X	0	0	200
Gymnasiarch on Delos	0	0	X	100
Agoranomos on Delos	X	0	0	100

Agoranomos on Delos	(X?)	0	0	100
ἐπὶ τὰ ἱερά	X	0	X	100
ἐπὶ τὰ ἱερά	[X]	0	X	100
Priest of Apollo on Delos	X	0	X	100
Priest of Artemis on the Island	0	0	X	100
Priest of Roma	(X?)	0	X	100
Priest of Anios	0	0	0	50
Priest of Sarapis on Delos	0	0	X	50
Priest of ἁγνῆς Ἀφροδίτης	X	0	X	100
Herald to Delos	0	0	0	100
Priest of Zeus Kynthios	0	0	X	100
Priest of Dionysos	0	0	0	50
Director of the Public Bank on Delos	X	0	0	200
Total number of contributors	24	14	24	62
Total amount contributed	2700 Dr.	1500 Dr.	2450 Dr.	6650 Dr.
Plus extraordinary contributions of:	Medeios 700 Dr.[5]		Sarapion 950 Dr.[6]	+1650 Dr.
				8300
Plus contributions of years I-IV				+10,750
Total amount contributed over the 7 year period				19,050 Dr.

The contributions of the last two years and the supplemental one never attained the numbers of the first three years. Payments, however, regularly came from Athenian officials and some of the leading Delian

---

[5]400 Dr. in contributions as Hoplite General and Epimeletes of Delos already counted.

[6]200 Dr. contribution as Hoplite General already counted.

officials. Only the minor officials of the Island and the priests failed to contribute regularly. Even with the extraordinary contributions of Medeios and Sarapion, the subscription of 99/8 and 98/7 ultimately fell some 300 drachmas short of the total projected sum of ca. 6100 drachmas for the biennium. It required the additional contribution of 2450 drachmas from the officials of 97/6 to bring the total for the seven year period to 19,050 drachmas, i.e. at or slightly over the projected goal (6 x ca. 3,000+ drachmas).

The lack of participation of the Delian officials of 98/7 seems particularly notable and suggests action in concert. Perhaps here we have some evidence in the year of the actual Pythaïs of rivalry between cults. The inclusion of the priests of Delos as the only priests required to contribute for the Pythaïs cannot have been justified. The evidence of the inscription suggests that they became increasingly unwilling to participate. They duly made their contributions in the third year, but late (*supra*, pp. 90,96) and probably, therefore, under some pressure. After that, they did not contribute for the most part until the supplementary effort of 97/6. Perhaps they were assured by then that a fairer way would be found for collecting the "first fruits" for the second enneëteric Pythaïs or, perhaps, someone influential, such as Sarapion, simply exerted the necessary pressure.

The officeholders listed above were expected to contribute for the Pythaïs; but whatever pressure was brought to bear on them to pay up was moral rather than legal, for a number simply neglected to do so. It appears in fact, that the inscription itself, i.e. publicizing the record, formed the chief means of pressuring people to make their payments. Whatever the financial obligations entailed, Athenians stood for the offices in sufficient numbers to enable the government to operate smoothly. There was no shortage of persons willing and financially able to stand; 121 separate individuals are known to have held office from the present inscription alone. At the same time, the evidence suggests that the obligations constituted a real financial burden in some cases. The very existence of a 50 drachma quota reveals that the persons holding offices assessed that amount could normally be expected to have relatively modest means. Perhaps 50 drachmas was a greater burden proportionally for them than 200 drachmas was for persons who had the means to stand for the Hoplite Generalship. We may suspect that this was the case, for the default rate is among the highest for those offices assessed 50 drachmas. In short the burdens appear to have been real and felt.

The need also must have been real; the creation of the stele itself shows that. The maintenance of good relations with Delphi apparently required that "first fruits" of approximately three talents be sent to Delphi with the "eight-year" Pythaïs. The legislation proposed by Xenotimos to meet the problem, however, must be characterized as unrealistic. The amount needed was about 3000 drachmas a year. The legislation made it a semi-voluntary liturgy of 31 officials to contribute the sum. However, in order to reach the required total, a nearly 100% rate of giving had to be maintained, for, if every official contributed in a given year, the total for each year would have come to 3250 drachmas. As long as times remained good and everyone was willing, things went as planned. But, as we have observed above in the section entitled "The Year Headings", times did not remain good nor did the priests remain willing for long; and people apparently could not be made to pay in times of stress.

THE OFFICES AND OFFICEHOLDERS

The text, charts, and discussions which precede reveal that a specified group of officials appears on II^2 2336. The list is not random, i.e. one official giving in one year and in no other, with the result that we have no idea from whom contributions were expected. On the contrary, it is sufficiently regular that we can establish from the first year a complete list of officials who were expected to give; officials from this list alone appear in the rest of the inscription.[1] They do not always contribute, but this is the regular list. Both Athenian and Delian officials appear. The language of the preamble defines them as...τοὺς δόντας τῶν ἀρχόντων τὰς ἀπαρχάς... (II^2 2336, line 3).[2]

The list appears to be a select one of senior officials elected or chosen annually to act as agents of the Demos.[3] Beyond the palpable fact that the most important officials known appear, the rationale behind

---

[1]The only exception being that both Medeios and Sarapion chose, in making their extraordinarily large donations, to give in their capacity as agonothetai of various games. The office of Agonothetes is otherwise not listed on II^2 2336; the usual contribution for this office was 250 drachmas.

[2]The word ἄρχων seems to be used here in the technical sense. For a discussion of the technical meaning of ἀρχή, see M.H. Hansen "Seven Hundred *Archai* in Classical Athens," *GRBS* 21 (1980) pp. 152-154.

[3]That the list is a selection rather than a complete one may be surmised from the attested existence ca. 100 B.C. of the Generals ἐπὶ τὸν Πειραιᾶ (II^2 2872, 2873, 2952, and *Hesperia* 36, 1967, p. 88, line 38), ἐπ' Ἴμβρον (*Hesperia* 36, 1967, p. 89, lines 41-44), and ἐπὶ Ῥαμνοῦντα καὶ τὴν παραλίαν χώραν (II^2 2869). These generals receive no mention on II^2 2336.

the selection remains somewhat obscure.[4] We may reasonably assume, however, that the offices listed on II^2 2336 are the more important rather than the less important ones.[5] While only some Athenian officials appear, it is a notable fact that all known annual officials of Delos, including the Delian priesthoods, are listed on II^2 2336.[6] Only the Priest of Asklepios and the Priest of the Great Gods (Kabiri) are missing. We do not need to look far for the reason. By the time of II^2 2336, the cult of Asklepios had apparently been absorbed by that of the Syrian deities,[7] while the priesthood of the Great Gods was, it would appear, no longer an annual office (*ID* 1562). In short, the wording

---

[4]Why, for example, does the Gymnasiarch on Delos appear, but no Athenian official connected with the ephebes?

[5]It is possible, for example, that the board of 10 generals was organized under three categories--1) infantry; 2) military supplies; 3) naval forces--and that the head of each arm only was required to give, namely the Hoplite General, the General ἐπὶ τὴν παρασκευήν, the General ἐπὶ τὸ ναυτικόν. The board certainly developed and changed (see Ferguson, "Researches III," *Klio* 9, 1909, p. 314ff.).

[6]Priesthoods were not usually *archai* in the technical sense (see Hansen, "Seven Hundred *Archai*...," *GRBS* 21, 1980, p. 153). These annual Delian priesthoods seem to have been an exception. Like the other offices listed on the stele, they were annual and could not, it appears, be held simultaneously with any other office.

[7]Roussel, *DCA* pp. 238-239; Bruneau, *Recherches sur les cultes de Délos*..., *Bibl. Ec. fr. Ath. et Rome*, fasc. 217 (Paris, 1970) pp. 376-377.

of the legislation proposed by Xenotimos (II^2 2336$_4$) must either have listed separately each office which was required to give or have specified that all officials of a certain category or categories were to contribute. The latter alternative seems the more practical. Xenotimos appears to have stipulated the most important annual officials of the city plus all the annual officials who served on Delos.

The titles of the officials vary to a surprising degree. Quite often considerations of space are manifestly the reason. When the title can be put in one line and the name in the next, the full form of the title tends to be used. When lack of space requires that the title and name be accommodated in one line, then shortened forms appear. Thus we find ναύαρχος (lines 19, 90, 146, 166) for στρατηγὸς ἐπὶ τὸ ναυτικόν (lines 222, 258, 266) and κῆρυξ 'Αρεοπαγιτῶν (once only in line 103) for the usual κῆρυξ βουλῆς τῆς ἐξ 'Αρείου πάγου. Considerations of spacing do not account for all variants, for ἐπιμελητὴς τοῦ ἐμ Πειραιεῖ λιμένος (lines 22, 86) and ἐπιμελητὴς Πειραιέως (lines 106, 235) are each accorded one full line with the name coming in the next line. We must conclude that titles were not as fixed as we would expect them to be and that it was possible to refer to the same official with two rather different titles, e.g. ἐπὶ τὴν φυλακὴν τῶν ἱερῶν χρημάτων and ἐπὶ τὰ ἱερά (see Roussel, DCA pp. 133-135). The practice of individuals clearly played its part as well. The following list summarizes all the titles and variants which occur on II^2 2336:

στρατηγὸς ἐπὶ τὰ ὅπλα (no variation)

κῆρυξ βουλῆς τῆς ἐξ 'Αρείου πάγου (lines 8, 150, 180, 190, 245), κῆρυξ 'Αρεοπαγιτῶν (line 103)

ἄρχων (no variation)

βασιλεύς (no variation)

πολέμαρχος (no variation)

θεσμοθέται (no variation)

ναύαρχος (lines 19, 90, 146, 166); στρατηγὸς ἐπὶ τὸ ναυτικόν (lines 222, 258, 266)

στρατηγὸς ἐπὶ τὴν παρασκευὴν τὴν ἐν ἄστει (lines 20, 88, 262); στρατηγὸς ἐπὶ τὴν παρασκευήν (lines 104, 178?, 215?)

ἐπιμελητὴς τοῦ ἐμ Πειραιεῖ λιμένος (lines 22, 86, 144); ἐπιμελητὴς Πειραιέως (lines 106, 220, 235)

ἐπιμελητὴς Δήλου (no variation)

[ἐπιμελητὴς ἐμπορίου] ἐν Δήλωι (line 65); ἐπιμελητὴς ἐμπορίου (line 110); ἐμπορίου ἐπιμελητής (line 176)

γυμνασίαρχος εἰς Δῆλον (lines 28, 117); γυμνασίαρχος εἰς τὸ ἐν Δήλωι γυμνάσιον (lines 73, 268)

ἀγορανόμοι εἰς Δῆλον (lines 30, 224); ἀγορανόμοι (lines 67, 112)

ἐπὶ τὴν φυλακὴν τῶν ἱερῶν χρημάτων (lines 33, 69, 232); ἐπὶ τὰ ἱερά (lines 114, 203, 217)

ἱερεὺς 'Απόλλωνος ἐν Δήλωι (no variation)

ἱερεὺς 'Αρτέμιδος ἐν νήσωι (no variation)

ἱερεὺς 'Ρώμης (no variation)

ἱερεὺς 'Ανίου (no variation)

ἱερεὺς Σαράπιδος ἐν Δήλωι (lines 42, 133, 260); ἱερεὺς Σαράπιδος (line 83)

ἱερεὺς ἁγνῆς θεοῦ (lines 43, 84); ἱερεὺς ἁγνῆς θεοῦ ἐν Δήλωι (line 131); ἱερεὺς ἁγνῆς 'Αφροδίτης ἐν Δήλωι (lines 218, 237)

κῆρυξ εἰς Δῆλον (no variation)

ἱερεὺς Διὸς Κυνθίου (lines 45, 85); ἱερεὺς Διὸς Κυνθίου ἐν Δήλῳ (line 241) ἱερεὺς Διονύσου (no variation)

ὁ ἐπὶ τὴν τράπεζαν τὴν ἐν Δήλωι (line 77); ἐπὶ τὴν δημοσίαν τράπεζαν τὴν ἐν Δήλωι (line 184); ὁ ἐπὶ τὴν δημοσίαν τράπεζαν τὴν ἐν Δήλωι (line 270)

These offices fall naturally into four groups as follows:

I. Group one comprises the officials who contributed 200 drachmas (namely the Hoplite General, the Epimeletes of Delos, the Epimeletes of Emporion, and the Director of the Public Bank on Delos) plus the Herald of the Areopagos. These offices were all elective positions. The incumbents, where we can judge their ages at all, were usually 50 years of age or older.[8] Their careers suggest that these were the most important administrative offices.[9] Membership in the Areopagos appears to have been a requirement for holding these offices.

II. The second group is composed of seven officials whose titles suggest that they exercised administrative duties with regard to commerce, military preparedness, and temple properties plus the Herald to Delos and the Gymnasiarch on Delos. These offices were all elective ones and apparently were open, at least in some cases, to individuals who had not yet become members of the Areopagos.

---

[8]The notable exceptions are Medeios of Piraeus and Polykleitos of Phlya, both of whom are attested as child pythaïsts at Delphi in 128/7 and must, therefore, have been in their early to middle forties in 100 B.C.

[9]An additional indication of the importance of the Hoplite General, the Epimeletes of Delos, and the Epimeletes of Emporion is that they are consistently listed first in their respective groups (supra, p. 86ff.).

III. The nine traditional Athenian Archons comprise group three. These offices were chosen by lot.

IV. The Priests of Delos make up group four.

In the following pages we shall examine the offices and the careers of the incumbents. N.B.: An asterisk precedes the name of any individual about whom nothing else is known except that he held the office listed on II^2 2336. Complete references and biographical data are provided for each individual in the prosopographical index.

* * * * *

Group I

A. Hoplite General; B. Herald of the Areopagos; C. Epimeletes of Delos; D. Epimeletes of Emporion; E. Director of the Public Bank on Delos.

A. Hoplite General

1.	103/2	Ammonios [Demetriou] Anaphlystios	line 6	XI	coastal[10]
2.	102/1	Sarapion Meliteus	line 51	VIII	city
3.	101/0	*Apollodoros Ḍ[_ _ _ _]	line 93	--	--
4.	100/99	Hestiaios Theokharidos ek Kerameon	line 139	VI	city
5.	99/8	[Medeios Medeiou] Peiraieus	line 165	IX	city
6.	98/7	Sarapion Sarapionos Meliteus	line 206	VIII	city
7.	97/6	Pyrrhos Pyrrhou Lamptreus	line 257	I	coastal

[10] I have followed the tables of J.S. Traill, _The Political Organization of Attica_, _Hesperia_ Suppl. 14 (Princeton, 1975) in the assignment of Tribes and Trittyes. The indication of Trittys has been omitted in uncertain cases, i.e. those by which Traill placed a question mark.

1. Epimeletes of Delos in 107/6; his brothers, Dionysios and Demetrios, held several priesthoods on the Island. The family, therefore, appears to have had strong Delian connections.

2, 6. Epimeletes of Delos in 100/99; leader of the Pythaïs in 98/7. A daughter and son were active in the cult of Delian Apollo, but this activity seems to belong only to the year of their father's Governorship.

4. Perhaps Agoranomos on Delos in 101/0. His cousin, Theokharis, was Herald of the Areopagos in 101/0 and ἐπὶ τὰ ἱερά on Delos in 99/8.

5. Eponymous Archon in 101/0, Director of the Public Bank on Delos in 100/99, Epimeletes of Delos in 98/7. His family has strong Delian connections; he was probably a resident of the Island.

7. Epimeletes of Delos in 104/3, Director of the Public Bank on Delos between 104/3 and 98/7, Herald of the Areopagos in 98/7. His family is a distinguished one with longstanding Delian connections.

Whatever the specific duties of the office,[11] the primacy of place

---

[11]On the office and its incumbents, see T. Sarikakis _The Hoplite General in Athens, A Prosopography_ (Chicago, 1976--unchanged version of Sarikakis' 1951 Princeton dissertation); pp. 17-21 deal with his duties. His primary concerns at this time were probably with military affairs (_Ath. Pol._ 61) and with the guaranteeing of the grain supply (T. Sarikakis, _Πλάτων_ 9, 1957, pp. 121-132). On the number and duties of the generals known in the second century B.C., see Ferguson "Researches III," _Klio_ 9 (1909) pp. 314-323; G. Busolt-M. Swoboda, _Griechische Staatskunde_ (Munich, 1926) p. 1121ff.; for the office in the years after Sulla, see Geagan, _The Athenian Constitution after Sulla_, pp. 18-31.

accorded it on this inscription and the careers of the men who held it (note that the Governorship of Delos was held by most of these men either soon before or soon after serving as Hoplite General) suggest that the Hoplite Generalship was the most important post in Athens at this time. The repeated tenure of Sarapion demonstrates that the office remained an elective one, as it had been from its inception.

The careers of these men also reveal that the Athenians in this period had no formalized *cursus honorum*.[12] The rise of Medeios (no. 5 above), however, provides us with some valuable evidence on another matter.[13] He held in rapid succession, and at a fairly youthful age, a series of high offices, but these were, it appears, preceded by his Eponymous Archonship, as though it were a requirement to the others. It seems probable, therefore, that membership in the Areopagos was expected, if not formally required, of those standing for election to the highest offices.[14] This had the advantage of guaranteeing that a candidate had

---

[12]Geagan's important and valuable study of *The Athenian Constitution after Sulla* is weakened by the (apparently unquestioned) assumption that the Athenians not only recognized the notion but actually used a formal *cursus honorum*. See the review of Geagan by J. and L. Robert, "Bulletin epigraphique," *REG* 82 (1969) p. 444 no. 153 and V. Ehrenberg, *Gnomon* 41 (1969) p. 594.

[13]On Medeios see also pp. 93-94 *supra* and pp. 160-164 *infra*.

[14]There are no known exceptions. J. Sundwall has suggested that this principle applied to the Governorship of Delos (*Untersuchungen über die Attischen Münzen des Neueren Stils* [*Oefversigt of Finska Vetenskaps - Societens Forhändlar* 45-50, 1906-8] Helsingfors 1908, p. 71) and E. Badian has reaffirmed it (*AJAH* 1, 1976, p. 107 and n. 10, 114 and n. 40.

at least some previous administrative experience. Beyond this, the Athenian system had a certain random quality (influenced by the practice of sortition?) and left much to the wealth, ambition, and personal connections of individuals.

B. Herald of the Council of the Areopagos

1.	103/2	Ḥẹ[_ _ _ _ _]	line 9	--	--
2.	102/1	not inscribed	lines 62-63	--	--
3.	101/0	Theokharis ek Kerameon	line 103	VI	city
4.	100/99	*[_ca._7_]ịstratos Sphettios	line 151	VI	inland
5.	99/8	Athenodoros Athenogenou Aixoneus	line 181	VIII	coastal
6.	98/7	Pyrrhos Pyrrhou Lamptreus	line 191	I	coastal
7.	97/6	Andreas Andreou [Peiraieus]	line 246	IX	city

3. Kosmetes of ephebes in Athens in 119/8 and ἐπὶ τὰ ἱερά on Delos in 99/8. His cousin, Hestiaios, was Hoplite General in 100/99.

5. His son is attested as Thesmothetes in 88/7.

6. Hoplite General in 97/6, q.v.

7. Adjunct member of the ephebic corps on Delos in 119/8, Epimeletes of Delos in ca. 90.

The Herald is usually listed in this inscription along with the nine traditional Archons, as though at the head of a board.[15] From the relative prominence of the three noted above, he must be considered a senior official, inferior in political power and influence only to the

---

[15]Lines 8, 150, 190, and 245 (supra, p. 86 and n. 1).

Hoplite General and the Governor of Delos (cf. Ferguson, Hellenistic Athens p. 429 n. 2). Apparently, already a member of the Areopagos, he was elected, presumably by his fellow members in the Council, to preside over the incoming board of Archons. The Council of the Areopagos thus had grown to a position of prominence by 103/2; it became predominant in the period after Sulla (Geagan, The Athenian Constitution after Sulla p. 41ff.).[16]

C. Epimeletes of Delos

1.	103/2	*[Dioskourides_ _ _ _]	line 25	--	--
2.	102/1	[Theodo]tos Sounieus	line 64	XII	coastal
3.	101/0	*Kallistratos [ca. 4]eus	line 109	--	--
4.	100/99	Sarapion Meliteus	line 141	VIII	city
5.	99/8	Polykleitos [Alexandrou Phly]eus	line 202	V	inland
6.	98/7	Medeios Medeiou Peiraieus	line 189	IX	city
7.	97/6	[Aristion] Sokratou ex Oiou	line 229	IV or XII	--

---

[16]Geagan (p. 61) observes: "Precisely when and how the Areopagus was raised to its predominant position in the Roman constitution is not clear." As Geagan recognizes, the prominence of the Areopagos and its Herald was not something new to Athens in 86 B.C. and after. As the city and its officials gained in power and prestige as a result of the growing commerce on Delos, the influence of the Areopagos naturally increased in the years after 166 B.C. (pp. 171-172 infra).

2. Priest of the Syrian Divinities on Delos ca. 113/2, Priest of Holy Aphrodite in 110/09.

4. Hoplite General in 102/1, q.v.

5. Child pythaïst in 128/7, Archon(?) in 110/09, knight in the Pythaïs of 106/5.

6. Hoplite General in 99/8, q.v.

7. Epimeletes of Emporion in 101/0; his father was Epimeletes of Delos in 117/6.

The Epimeletes of Delos headed the administration of the Island. The office appears to have been an elective one, for almost everyone who held the post of Hoplite General in this period also served as Epimeletes of Delos.[17]

Of the incumbents listed above, three--Theodotos, Medeios, and Aristion--have notable Delian associations over a number of years.

D. Epimeletes of Emporion

1.	103/2	Ị[_ _ _ _ _]	line 27	--	--
2.	102/1	[_ _ca _16 _ _ _ _]ṣ	line 66	--	--
3.	101/0	Aristion ex Oiou	line 111	IV or XII	--

---

[17]See also Roussel's admirable discussion of the office and known incumbents in DCA pp. 97-125. His deduction that the Epimeletes had no military function (p. 125), however, appears suspect. It is difficult to suppose, in light of the troubled times around 100 B.C., particularly the slave revolt, that men who had held the Hoplite Generalship would not have had some say in the protection of the Island.

4.	100/99	not recorded		--	--
5.	99/8	Arkhias Diogenou Ana[phlystios]	line 177	XI	coastal
6.	98/7	not recorded on II^2 2336			
		(Dionysios Athenobiou Eupyrides	ID 1711	IV	inland)
7.	97/6	not recorded		--	--

3. Epimeletes of Delos in 97/6, q.v.

5. General ἐπὶ τὸ ναυτικόν, probably in 101/0.

6. NPA p. 59, stemma p. 7: child pythaïst in 128/7 (FD III 2 no. 12, line 5), honored with a crown by the Athenians in ca. 100 (Hesperia Suppl. 15 p. 73 no. 14), mint magistrate in 97/6 with his brother, Νικήτης, who is attested as an ephebe in 117/6 (II^2 1009, line 65).[18]

This official had surveillance over the harbor and the transhipment of goods, and probably also over weights and measures (Roussel, DCA pp. 179-182). The office probably required some specialized knowledge in the areas of shipping and finance since, of the six known incumbents (for the entire list, see Roussel, DCA p. 181), one, Arkhias, is attested as General ἐπὶ τὸ ναυτικόν; another, Dionysios, as an Athenian mint magistrate; and a third, Lysimakhos, as ὁ ἐπὶ τὰ ἱερά on Delos in 97/6 (ID 1878). Originally a board of three (ID 1507, lines 16-18), by the time of II^2 2336 the powers of the board had been concentrated in one man. The resulting office, the 200 drachma contribution and the position of precedence in the list reveal, was a senior one superior to the harbor

---

[18]D.M. Lewis, "The Chronology of the Athenian New Style Coinage," NC 7th Series 2 (1962) p. 289.

officials of Piraeus.[19]

E. Director of the Public Bank on Delos

1.	103/2	not recorded		--	--
2.	102/1	*Kallias Athmoneus	line 78	XII	inland
3.	101/0	not recorded		--	--
4.	100/99	Medeios Medeiou Peiraieus	line 185	IX	city
5.	99/8?	Py[rrh]os Pyrrhou Lamptreus	line 271	I	coastal
6.	98/7	not recorded		--	--
7.	97/6	not recorded		--	--

4. Hoplite General in 99/8, q.v. The date of his service as Director of the Bank is not independently known, but may be inferred (supra, p. 94).

5. Hoplite General in 97/6, q.v. The date of Pyrrhos' incumbency cannot be determined with certainty. The years 103/2 and 101/0 are also possible.

The incumbents come from distinguished families and have prominent Delian connections. The two other men who are known to have held the

---

[19]The qualification of this office with the phrase ἐν Δήλωι in line 65 (see commentary ad loc.) clearly differentiates it from the office of ἐπιμελητὴς Πειραιέως (line 106 e.g.). R. Stroud (Hesperia 43, 1974, p. 181 n. 92) failed to realize that the ἐπιμελητὴς ἐμπορίου listed on II[2] 2336 is the Delian official of that title and not the Athenian one, which was probably no longer in existence at this date.

office, Theodoros son of Straton of Marathon[20] and Diogenes son of Aropos of Piraeus (ID 1670), fit the pattern--the first was ἐπὶ τὴν φυλακὴν τῶν ἱερῶν χρημάτων on Delos (ID 1416 B, col. I, line 3), the other was Epimeletes of the Island (ID 1839). The specific duties of the post are unknown, but the careers of the men who held it and the 200 drachma assessment reveal its importance.[21]

* * * * *

Group II

A. Epimeletes of the Harbor in Piraeus; B. General ἐπὶ τὸ ναυτικόν ; C. General ἐπὶ τὴν παρασκευήν ; D. Agoranomoi on Delos; E. οἱ ἐπὶ τὰ ἱερά ; F. Herald to Delos; G. Gymnasiarch on Delos.

A. Epimeletes of the Harbor in Piraeus

1.	103/2	Demeas Ha[laieus]	line 23	II or VIII	coastal
2.	102/1	Buttakos Lamptreus	line 87	I	coastal
3.	101/0	Kephisodoros Aixoneus	line 107	VIII	coastal
4.	100/99	*Dionysios Palleneus	line 145	XI	inland
5.	99/8?	[ca. 5]ọ[1-2]ṭḥeos Kh[_ _ _]	line 221	--	--
6.	98/7	not recorded		--	--
7.	97/6	[_ _ ca. 16_ _ _]es	line 236	--	--

1. Epimeletes of Delos ca. 90 B.C. Members of his family served as mint magistrates and as priests.

---

[20] ID 1421 Ab, lines 9-10; note that the office is described as elective.

[21] See Roussel, DCA pp. 139, 176-178.

2. Gymnasiarch on Delos in 104/3. His brother Pyrrhos was Hoplite General in 97/6, q.v.

3. General on Imbros in ca. 100.

This official apparently supervised the maritime trade in the Piraeus. The office is attested for the first time in 112/1, when its recently elected occupant was honored by an association of sea merchants (II² 1012), and is perhaps also mentioned in connection with establishing weights and measures in ca. 100 B.C. (II² 1013, line 40). The office may have been newly established as an indirect result of the growth of commerce on Delos and replaced, almost certainly, the Athenian board of ten Epimeletai of Emporion (p. 45 *supra*).

B. Nauarch or General ἐπὶ τὸ ναυτικόν

1.	103/2	*Kephis[_ _ _ _ _]	line 19	--	--
2.	102/1	Python Meliteus	line 90	VIII	city
3.	101/0?	Arkhias Diogenou Anaphlystios	line 259	XI	coastal
4.	100/99	Theon Paionides	line 146	IV	inland
5.	99/8	[ca. 5] Euonymeus	line 166	I	city
6.	98/7	[Kharia]s Khariou Aithalides	line 223	IV	--
7.	97/6?	*Arkh[ias] Arkhestratou Kydathenaieus	line 267	III	city

The question marks signify that these dates are uncertain; the only alternative is that they be reversed, for the dates of the others seem reliable. Let us add that there was only one General ἐπὶ τὸ ναυτικόν in any given year.

2. As a child he took part in festivals on Delos in ca. 130 and 127/6; his father is known from a Delian catalog. Probably the family was resident on the Island.

3. Epimeletes of Emporion on Delos in 99/8.

4. ἐπὶ τὰ ἱερά in 109/8.

6. As a child he participated in a festival on Delos in ca. 130. He was ἐπὶ τὰ ἱερά in 97/6 and is also attested as Agoranomos on Delos and as paymaster of his prytany in Athens. His father and uncle are attested on Delos in about the year 150. His family appears to be Delian.

It is significant that the incumbents of this office who are attested elsewhere have connections of long standing both with Delos and with commercial affairs. We may infer that the person who held the office in this period was primarily concerned with the navy as a vital part of an economy based on maritime trade. The career of Ἵππαρχος Τιμοκλέους Πειραιεύς, General ἐπὶ τὸ ναυτικόν in 128/7 (FD III 2 no. 24, line 4), reveals the same pattern of association with the Island, for he was Epimeletes of the Island in 114/3 (ID 1901, 2165, 2208) and his daughter is attested in the service of Artemis on Delos about the same time (ID 1868).

C. General ἐπὶ τὴν παρασκευήν

1.	103/2	*Jas[on _ _ _ _]	line 21	--	--
2.	102/1	*Timoukhos Rhamnousios	line 89	X	coastal
3.	101/0	Dionysogenes Anagyrasios	line 105	I	coastal

4.	100/99	not recorded		--	--
5.	99/8	Dionysios Demetriou Aixoneus	line 179	VIII	coastal
6.	98/7	[ca. 9]s Dio[_ _ _ _ _]	line 216	--	--
7.	97/6?	*Agathokles Sosikratou Oinaios	line 263	V or XII	coastal

The question mark signifies that this last date is uncertain. It is possible that the entry in line 263 is a late contribution by the man who held office in 100/99.

3. His son is attested on Delos as a pompostolos in ca. 100 B.C.

5. His brother Demetrios was active on Delos as Priest of Roma in 101/0 and as Gymnasiarch in 98/7.

It appears to be significant that the incumbents of this office are almost unknown outside of this inscription. The small contribution expected of this official also suggests that the office was a relatively low-level one, perhaps held by young men. Dionysogenes, for example, was probably little more than 40 years of age when he held this office. Ferguson (Klio 9, 1909, pp. 319-320) discusses the office and interprets its close association with temple inventories (II^2 1539; II^2 839, lines 28-29; II^2 840, line 12) as evidence that temples were used in part as military storehouses.[22]

D. Agoranomoi on Delos

1a.	103/2	[Kikhe]sias Sounieus	line 31	XII	coastal
b.		*Hermokles [_ _ _ _ _]	line 32	--	--

[22]See also Busolt-Swoboda, Griechische Staatskunde, p. 1123 n. 1.

2a.	102/1	[ca.6]os Marathonios	line 67	X	coastal
b.		[ca.16]os	line 68	--	--
3a.	101/0	[ca.4]ios ek Kerameon	line 113	VI	city
b.		*Alexandros	line 113	--	--
4a.	100/99	not recorded		--	--
b.		not recorded		--	--
5a.	99/8?	[ca.9] Xypetaion	line 225	VIII	city
b.		[De]ṃ[et]rios Theodosiou Lakiades	line 226	VII	city
6a.	98/7	not recorded		--	--
b.		not recorded		--	--
7a.	97/6	not recorded		--	--
b.		not recorded		--	--

1a. His sons are known as pompostoloi on Delos in ca. 100.

3a. Probably to be identified with the Hoplite General of 100/99, q.v.

5b. The Eponymous Archon of 100/99 may be his brother.

Delian inscriptions provide us with the names of three others who served as Agoranomos around 100 B.C.: Kharias of Aithalidai, Nauarch in 98/7 (q.v.); Ekhedemos of Sounion, Priest of Asklepios on Delos in ca. 117 (ID 1834) and from a family which was active on the Island (NPA p. 83); and Sokrates of Kephisia, PA 13113 (ID 1835), Priest of Apollo on Delos (ID 1936). The incumbents, thus, seem to be residents of the Island and men of some consequence. Nothing is known of their precise duties beyond what can be inferred from their title (see Roussel, DCA pp.

182-184).[23]

E. οἱ ἐπὶ τὰ ἱερά

1a.	103/2	*Theotimos Aixoneus	line 34	VIII	coastal
b.		Xenokles Rhamnousios	line 35	X	coastal
2a.	102/1	[_ _ _ _ _]	line 70	--	--
b.		*[_ _ _]mokritos Akharneus	line 70	VII	inland
3a.	101/0	*Deinias Palleneus	line 115	XI	inland
b.		*Philemon	line 116	--	--
4a.	100/99	not recorded		--	--
b.		not recorded		--	--
5a.	99/8	Theo[kharis Hestiaiou ek Kera]meon	line 203	VI	city
b.		Diopha[ntos Aristokleous Marathonios]	line 217	X	coastal
6a.	98/7	not recorded		--	--
b.		not recorded		--	--
7a.	97/6	[Lysimakhos Aristeidou] Hestiaiothen	line 233	II	city
b.		[Kharias Khariou] Aithalides	line 234	IV	--

1b. Thesmothetes in 100/99. This reveals that this post was open, at least in some cases, to those who were not yet members of the Areopagos.

5a. Herald of the Council of the Areopagos in 101/0, q.v.

---

[23]See also P.V. Stanley, "Agoranomoi and Metronomoi: Athenian Market Officials and Regulations," Ancient World 2 (1979) pp. 13-18 for a discussion of the number and duties of the Athenian Agoranomoi in the fourth century B.C. The Delian office was probably modelled on the Athenian; how much the duties had changed in two centuries, it is impossible to say.

5b. Priest of the Holy Goddess in 103/2 and Priest of Zeus Kynthios in 94/3.

7a. Epimeletes of Emporion in ca. 94. Delian family.

7b. Nauarch in 98/7, q.v.

Many incumbents are known thanks to the survival on stone of the temple inventories which they compiled. They come from all political levels. Roussel (DCA pp. 135-138) gives a complete list which confirms this. Theokharis (5a) notwithstanding, persons of well-known families usually hold this office early in their careers. This was an important lower echelon office, which dealt primarily with temple accounts and records (see especially DCA pp. 133-135).

F. Herald to Delos

1.	103/2	Glaukias Krioeus	line 44	XI	--
2.	102/1	*Philon Paianieus	line 91	III	inland
3.	101/0	*Myron Leukonoeus	line 120	IV	--
4.	100/99	*Philomeleidas Kydathenaieus	line 143	III	city
5.	99/8	not recorded		--	--
6.	98/7	not recorded		--	--
7.	97/6	not recorded		--	--

1. Participated in the Pythaïs of 98/7 as a Dionysiac artist. His father was also prominent in the guild of Dionysiac artists.

Although the duties of this office are unclear, it is notable that one, and perhaps two (see the prosopographical index on Myron of Leukonoion), of the four known incumbents were members of the guild of

Dionysiac artists. His position in the list, either among the priests or just before them, suggests that he may be a sacred herald. It appears that he was chosen by some other manner than sortition.[24]

G. Gymnasiarch on Delos

1.	103/2	*Metrodoros Kydathenaieus	line 29	III	city
2.	102/1	[_ _ _ _ _ _]	line 74	--	--
3.	101/0	*Dionysodoros Deiradiotes	line 118	IV	coastal
4.	100/99	not recorded		--	--
5.	99/8	not recorded		--	--
6.	98/7	not recorded on II[2] 2336			
		(Demetrios Demetriou Aixoneus	ID 1929	VIII	coastal)
7.	97/6	Damon Ikarieus	line 269	XII	inland

6. Priest of Roma in 101/0, q.v.

7. ἐπὶ τὰ ἱερά on Delos ca. 92 B.C.

This official fulfilled the same function as the Kosmetes of ephebes in Athens (ID 2594 and 2598) and was also in charge of athletic contests at the various festivals (ID 2596 e.g.). It was an elective office (ID 2589, line 36) and, in a practical sense, one of the most important in the everyday life of the Islanders. This explains why most of the incumbents (see ID 2589 for the list) appear to have been permanent residents on the Island (Roussel, DCA p. 186ff.).

---

[24]See also the κῆρυξ τοῦ θεοῦ listed in FD III 2 no. 6, line 17 = Hesperia Suppl. 15 p. 49 and K. Clinton's discussion of the sacred herald at Eleusis in "The Sacred Officials of the Eleusinian Mysteries," Trans. Am. Philosoph. Soc. 64 (1974) pp. 76, 81-82.

* * * *

Group III

A. Archon; B. Basileus; C. Polemarch; D. Thesmothetai

A. Archon

1.	103/2	*Theokles	lines 5, 10	--	--
2.	102/1	*Ekhekrates [Trinem]ẹeus	lines 49, 52	VIII	inland
3.	101/0	Medeios Peiraieus	lines 92, 94	IX	city
4.	100/99	Theodosios Lakiades	lines 137, 152	VII	city
5.	99/8	*Prokles	lines 163, 167, 239	--	--
6.	98/7	Argeios Argeiou Trikorysios	lines 192, 204	X	coastal
7.	97/6	*Herakleitos Heṛ[ca. 7 _] Sphettios	line 247	VI	inland

3. Hoplite General in 99/8, q.v.

4. This man is probably the Priest of Apollo Patroös attested in II^2 2871; his brother or son, Demetrios, perhaps participated in the Pythaïs of 98/7 as a Dionysiac artist and is also known from II^2 2336, line 226 as Agoranomos(?).

6. ἐπὶ τὰ ἱερά in 109/8; General ἐπὶ τὸν Πειραιᾶ in ca. 100 B.C. and *ex officio* Archetheoros of the Pythaïs of 98/7.

The incumbents of this office are surprisingly obscure, perhaps because they were chosen by lot. Four are known only in their capacity as Eponymous Archon; only Medeios and, to a lesser extent, Argeios, left a significant mark outside of his service as Archon. The office undoubtedly carried some prestige in that the holder gave his name to the year; but the duties in this period may have been primarily ceremonial. On his duties, see Ath. Pol. 56.

B. Basileus

1.	103/2	[_ _ _ _ _]	line 11	--	--
2.	102/1	[_ca._11_]s Sounieus	line 71	XII	coastal
3.	101/0	Herodotos Probalisios	line 95	XII	coastal
4.	100/99	Kallimakhos Leukonoeus	line 153	IV	--
5.	99/8	[_ _ _ _ _]	line 168	--	--
6.	98/7	Arkhonides Naukratou ek Kerameon	line 193	VI	city
7.	97/6	*Ariston P̣[antak]leous Gargettios	line 248	II	inland

3. Pythaïst in 98/7.

4. Mint magistrate in 93/2. His family became very prominent in Athens in the years after 86 B.C., his son becoming Herald of the Areopagos, his grandson Epimeletes of Delos, and his great-grandson priest in the Genos of the Kerykes.

6. Pythaïst ἐκ Κηρύκων in 106/5. His brother, Nausistratos, was ἐπὶ τὰ ἱερά on Delos in 110/09.

This office clearly retained its traditional religious duties; thus, members of the ancient Genos of the Κήρυκες are prominent among the incumbents (Ath. Pol. 57).

C. Polemarch

1.	103/2	[_ _ _ _ _]	line 12	--	--

2.	102/1	*Diotimos Marathonios	line 54	X	coastal
3.	101/0	*Antipatros Kydathenaieus	line 96	III	city
4.	100/99	*Sosigenes Elaiousios	line 154	IX	--
5.	99/8	[_ _ _ _ _]	line 169	--	--
6.	98/7	Aristion Eudoxou Meliteus	line 194	VIII	city
7.	97/6	Antikrates [Philiskou] Epikephisios	line 249	VII	city

6. Ephebe in 128/7, Priest of Sarapis in 114/3. He was 48 years of age when he served as Polemarch.

7. Priest of Apollo on Delos in 101/0.

The fact that the two incumbents of this office attested elsewhere were priests suggests that the traditional religious duties of the office continued in this period (Ath. Pol. 58).

D. Thesmothetai

103/2

1.	[_ _ _ _ _]	line 13	--	--
2.	*Nik[ias]	line 14	--	--
3.	*Meidias	line 15	--	--
4.	*Dositheos	line 16	--	--
5.	*Dionysios Kh[_ _ _ _]	line 17	--	--
6.	*Apollonios	line 18	--	--

102/1

1.	Aristonymos Eleusinios	line 56	IX	coastal
2.	*Theon Erkhieus	line 57	II	inland

3.	*Bakkhios Akharneus	line 58	VII	inland
4.	*Alkibiades Potamios	line 59	IV	coastal
5.	*Pantakles Berenikides	line 60	V	--
6.	*Theopompos Kephalethen	line 61	VI	coastal

1. Proposer of a decree in Athens in 106/5; General ἐπὶ τὸν Πειραιᾶ in ca. 100.

101/0

1.	*[ca. 5]os Euonymeus	line 98	I	city
2.	*Artemidoros Berenikides	line 99	V	--
3.	*Phylotimos Kikynneus	line 100	VI	inland
4.	*Apollonides Lakiades	line 101	VII	city
5.	*Poplios Halaieus	line 102	VIII	coastal
6.	not recorded		--	--

100/99

1.	*Timotheos Kephisieus	line 155	I	inland
2.	Dositheos eg Myrrhinouttes	line 156	II	--
3.	*Menandros Paianieus	line 157	III	inland
4.	*Sosos Phlyeus	line 158	V	inland
5.	Xenokles Rhamnousios	line 159	X	coastal
6.	*Laphaes Sounieus	line 160	XII	coastal

2. From a family with prominent Delian connections, his uncle was Hierope of the Apollonia on Delos in 143/2; his son became Epimeletes of Delos in ca. 85.

5. ἐπὶ τὰ ἱερά in 103/2.

99/8

1.	[_ _ _ _ _]	line 170	--	--
2.	[_ca.6 _]SO[_ _]	line 171	--	--
3.	[ca.3]on Phlyeus	line 172	V	inland
4.	[ca.4_]krates Kholargeus	line 173	VI	city
5.	[ca.4_]les Thriasios	line 174	VII	coastal
6.	*Nausistratos Eroiades	line 175	IX or XI	--

98/7

1.	Apollonios Nikandrou Kytherrhios	line 195	III	--
2.	*Skamandrios Olympikhou Aphidnaios	line 196	V	inland
3.	Phileas Ephorou Pteleasios	line 197	VII	city
4.	Philion Philionos Eleusinios	line 198	IX	coastal
5.	Boulon Leostratou Palleneus	line 199	XI	inland
6.	Lakrateides Sostratou Ikarieus	line 200	XII	inland

1. Proxenos and euergetes of the inhabitants of Thera.

3. His father, Ephoros, is attested as Priest of Zeus Soter on Delos in 158/7 and was probably a member of the original cleruchy in 166/5.

4. Secretary of the Demos in 101 B.C.

5. Child pythaïst in the Pythaïs of 128/7 and a knight in the Pythaïs of 106/5.

6. Attested at Eleusis ca. 110 B.C. as ἱερεὺς θεοῦ καὶ θεᾶς καὶ Εὐβουλέως.

97/6

1.	Nikonomos [_ca.7_] ek Kedon	line 251	I	coastal
2.	*Diogenes [ca.4_] Kydathenaieus	line 252	III	city
3.	*Demetrios D[ca.6_] Paionides	line 253	IV	inland
4.	*Kleitomakhos [ca. 7 _] Phlyeus	line 254	V	inland
5.	Zenon Aristonos Marathonios	line 255	X	coastal
6.	Argeios A[sklapionos] Ateneus	line 256	XII	coastal

1. Third mint magistrate of ca. 109 B.C.

5. His brother, Ariston, was Gymnasiarch on Delos in 118/7. His brother's grandson rose to be Epimeletes of Delos in ca. 50 B.C.

6. Attested as a proposer of a decree in Athens in ca. 120 B.C.

Few of the men who served in this office achieved any real prominence, at least in our evidence. The highest posts attained were that of ὁ ἐπὶ τὰ ἱερά and third mint magistrate. The office appears to have been a low-level one primarily concerned with the courts (Ath. Pol. 59). The year of the Pythaïs was an attractive year to hold office, for men of greater stature than usual stood in 98/7, presumably so that they could participate in the Pythaïs in an official capacity.

The tribal affiliation of the board of Archons (see Table 1) reveals that these offices were allotted by a system which ensured that no more than one Archon in a given year came from the same tribe. Even with regard to the Herald of the Council of the Areopagos, there seems to have existed some tendency to avoid duplication, for it appears to be more than coincidental that his tribe duplicates that of another member only in 101/0. Thesmothetai were normally listed in tribal order; only in the second year is this not so.

TABLE 1
TRIBAL AFFILIATION OF THE NINE ARCHONS
AND THE HERALD OF THE AREOPAGOS

	Archon	Basileus	Polemarch	Thesmothetai						Herald of the Areopagos
103/2	-	-	-	-	-	-	-	-	-	-
102/1	VIII	XII	X	IX	II	VII	IV	V	VI	-
101/0	IX	XII	III	I	V	VI	VII	VIII	-	VI
100/99	VII	IV	IX	I	II	III	V	X	XII	VI
99/8	-	-	-	-	-	V	VI	VII	IX or XI	VIII
98/7	X	VI	VIII	III	V	VII	IX	XI	XII	I
97/6	VI	II	VII	I	III	IV	V	X	XII	IX

* * * *

Group IV: Delian Priests[25]

A. Priest of Apollo; B. Priest of Artemis on the Island; C. Priest of Roma; D. Priest of Anios; E. Priest of Dionysos; F. Priest of Sarapis; G. Priest of Holy Aphrodite; H. Priest of Zeus Kynthios

A. Priest of Apollo

1. 103/2 Ammonios Pambotades line 37 I --

---

[25]On the Delian cults and priesthoods in general, see Bruneau, *Recherches sur les cultes de Délos*, *Bibl. Ec. fr. Ath. et Rome*, fasc. 217 (Paris, 1970) and Roussel, *DCA* pp. 199-270.

2.	102/1	[_ ca.7_]ịon [_ _ _]	line 76	--	--
3.	101/0	Antikrates Epikephisios	line 122	VII	city
4.	100/99	Demetrios Demetriou Anaphlystios	lines 148-149	XI	coastal
5.	99/8	Protogenes Philades	line 240	II	coastal
6.	98/7	not recorded		--	--
7.	97/6	*[_ ca.8_]nos ex Oiou	line 231	IV or XII	--

1. His grandfather was one of the original cleruchs to Delos in 166/5.

3. Prominent on Delos in ca. 110; Polemarch in 97/6, a fact which reveals incidentally that one did not have to be a member of the Areopagos to serve as the major Priest on Delos.

4. Priest of Sarapis in 111/0. From a distinguished family, both of his brothers served as Epimeletes of Delos and as Hoplite General in the years 111 to 100 B.C.

5. Priest of Sarapis in 106/5.

This office was certainly the leading one among the priesthoods of the Island. Indicative of this is that two of the four known incumbents, as though in preparation, held another Delian priesthood, in both cases that of Sarapis. It is significant that these priests do not seem to have cultivated a secular career, though the offices held by Διονύσιος Δημητρίου 'Αναφλύστιος, brother of number 4, show that it was at least possible. He served as Priest of Apollo sometime before 111 (ID 1959), Epimeletes of Delos in 111/0 (ID 2125) and Hoplite General in 106/5 (FD III 2 no. 5, line 12).

B. Priest of Artemis on the Island

1.	103/2	Agathokles Ankylethen	line 39	II	city
2.	102/1	Theomnestos Kydathenaieus	line 82	III	city
3.	101/0	Philokles [Koloneth]en	line 124	IV	--
4.	100/99	not recorded		--	--
5.	99/8	not recorded		--	--
6.	98/7	not recorded		--	--
7.	97/6	*Marsyas Marsyou Meliteus	line 244	VIII	city

1. His son is attested on Delos in ca. 100 B.C.

2. Priest of Sarapis on Delos in 105/4.

3. Celebrant of the Hermaia in ca. 125; Paidotribes on Delos in 104/3 and in Athens in 97/6.

The incumbents of this office all appear to have strong connections with the Island which suggests that they resided there.

C. Priest of Roma[26]

1.	103/2	Pythilaos Sounieus	line 40	XII	coastal
2.	102/1	[ca. 10]eios	line 72	--	--
3.	101/0	Demetrios Aixoneus	line 128	VIII	coastal
4.	100/99	not recorded		--	--
5.	99/8?	*Leostratos Philokratou Phylasios	line 227	VII	coastal

---

[26]On the cult of Roma on Delos, see R. Mellor, ΘΕΑ ΡΩΜΗ, _The Worship of the Goddess Roma in the Greek World_, _Hypomnemata_ 42 (Göttingen, 1975) pp. 63-67.

6.	98/7	not recorded		--	--
7.	97/6	Demetrios Asklepidou Halaieus	line 265	II or VIII	coastal

Line 227 is perhaps to be dated to 98/7.

1. Ephebe in 128/7 in Athens.

3. Gymnasiarch on Delos in 98/7; the family appears to be Delian.

7. His cousins are attested as Priest of Dionysos in 101/0 and as Epimeletes of Piraeus in 103/2.

D. Priest of Anios

1.	103/2	*Timon Skambonides	line 41	IV	city
2.	102/1	Sarapion Aigilieus	line 80	V	coastal
3.	101/0	*Nymphodoros ek Kerameon	lines 129-130	VI	city
4.	100/99	not recorded		--	--
5.	99/8	not recorded		--	--
6.	98/7	not recorded		--	--
7.	97/6	not recorded		--	--

2. Priest of Zeus Kynthios in 99/8; his family clearly has long standing connections with Delos.

E. Priest of Dionysos

1.	103/2	vacat	line 46	--	--
2.	102/1	*Theodotos [_ _ _]	line 79	--	--
3.	101/0	Asklepiades [Halai]eus	line 126	II or VIII	coastal
4.	100/99	not recorded		--	--

5.	99/8	not recorded		--	--
6.	98/7	not recorded on II^2 2336			
		(Polemaios Athmoneus	ID 2400	XII	inland)
7.	97/6	not recorded		--	--

3. Attested as a dramatic poet in ca. 90 B.C. and mint magistrate ca. 103 B.C. His cousin served as Priest of Roma in 97/6.

6. His father Πολεμαῖος was Paidotribes on Delos in 118/7 (ID 1947, 1925) and in charge of the Nymphaion in 115/4 (ID 1839).

F. Priest of Sarapis[27]

1.	103/2	Drakon (Phlyeus)	line 42	V	inland
2.	102/1	*A[ca.4]ẹs Thorikios	line 83	VI	coastal
3.	101/0	Theobios Dionysiou Akharneus	line 134	VII	inland
4.	100/99	not recorded on II^2 2336			
		(*Kydenor Dionysiou Meliteus	ID 2093[28]	VIII	city)
5.	99/8	not recorded			
6.	98/7	not recorded on II^2 2336			
		(*Leon Agatharkhou Marathonios	ID 2105[28]	X	coastal)
7.	97/6	*Euktimenos [Eude]mou Eiteaios	line 261	XI	inland

---

[27]On the cult, see P. Roussel, Les cultes égyptiens à Délos (Paris, 1916).

[28]Dinsmoor, The Archons of Athens pp. 244-245, first made these assignments.

1. From a Delian family; his grandfather was one of the original settlers in 166/5.

3. Priest of Holy Aphrodite in 99/8 or 98/7 and Zeus Kynthios in 97/6.

G. Priest of Holy Aphrodite

1.	103/2	Diophantos Marathonios	line 43	X	coastal
2.	102/1	*Thea[ca.6] Ạng[elethen]	line 84	III	coastal
3.	101/0	Aristonous Protarkhous Sphettios	line 132	VI	inland
4.	100/99	not recorded on II[2] 2336			
		(*Philokles Zenonos Sphettios	ID 2237	VI	inland)
5.	99/8?	Theobios Dionysiou Akharneus	line 219	VII	inland
6.	98/7	not recorded		--	--
7.	97/6	Gaios [Gaiou Akharneus]	line 238	VII	inland

It is possible that Theobios served in 98/7.

1. ἐπὶ τὰ ἱερά in 99/8 and Priest of Zeus Kynthios in 94/3.

3. Third mint magistrate in 88/7. His son is attested as an ephebe in Athens in 102/1.

5. Priest of Sarapis in 101/0 and of Zeus Kynthios in 97/6.

7. His father was Priest of the Great Gods in 128/7 and of Sarapis in 115/4.

The close connection of this cult with that of Sarapis and of Zeus Kynthios seems notable.

H. Priest of Zeus Kynthios

1.	103/2	Zenon Kephisieus	line 45	I	inland
2.	102/1	*Demetrios [_ _ _]	line 85	--	--
3.	101/0	not recorded		--	--
4.	100/99	not recorded on II² 2336			
		(*Athenogenes Tisarkhou Halimousios	*ID* 2364	IV	city)
5.	99/8	not recorded on II² 2336			
		(Sarapion Sotadou Aigilieus	*ID* 1886	V	coastal)
6.	98/7	not recorded		--	--
7.	97/6	Theobios Dionysiou Akharneus	line 242	VII	inland

1. His son was ὑφιερεύς of Sarapis in 109/8 and kleidoukhos of Holy Aphrodite in 107/6; the family is prominent on Delos.

5. Priest of Anios in 102/1; his father is attested as Agoranomos on Delos ca. 150 and as Paidotribes in 133/2.

7. Priest of Sarapis in 101/0 and of Holy Aphrodite in 99/8.

* * *

TABLE 2

REPRESENTATION BY TRIBES

	Group I	Group II	Group III	Group IV	Total
I. Erechtheis	3	3	3	2	11
II. Aigeis	0	1	3	2	6
III. Pandionis	0	4	4	2	10
IV. Leontis	1	5	3	3	12
V. Ptolemaiis	1	0	6	3	10
VI. Akamantis	3	2	5	4	14
VII. Oineis	0	2	6	6	14
VIII. Kekropis	4	6	3	3	16
IX. Hippothontis	4	0	4	0	8
X. Aiantis	0	4	4	2	10
XI. Antiochis	2	4	1	2	9
XII. Attalis	2	2	5	2	11

The spread reflects a system which was designed to ensure that each tribe had its share of officeholders.

TABLE 3

REPRESENTATION OF CITY, COASTAL, AND INLAND DEMES

Group I			Group II			Group III		
city	coastal	inland	city	coastal	inland	city	coastal	inland
9	7	4	10	15	6	11	15	15

Group IV			Total		
city	coastal	inland	city	coastal	inland
8	13	10	38	50	35

The slight preponderance in the number of representatives from coastal demes may be significant, or it may indicate nothing more than that large numbers of people in Attica live and work near the sea. What does seem significant in these figures is that the system of sortition (visible in Group III and, to some extent, in IV) resulted in a relatively greater representation of inland demes and coastal demes as compared to city demes.[29] This over-representation (if that is what it should be called) is nicely redressed by the elective offices where the city demes tend to have by comparison more representatives. This hardly seems accidental--it would appear that the creators of the original system recognized that members of city demes would have a natural advantage in standing for the elective offices.

---

[29]Traill (Hesperia Suppl. 14 p. 71) has noted this fact with regard to representation in the Boule.

* * * *

The offices in Groups I and II appear to have been sought by the leading figures of the day, many of whom held more than one of them. Medeios of Piraeus and Sarapion of Melite, for example, together held six of the most senior posts (those in Group I) during the seven year period covered by II^2 2336. We may surmise, therefore, that these offices provided the chief arena of political and financial power.

The offices in Group III, chosen by lot, were held, with very few exceptions, by persons whose careers are obscure to us.[30] In many cases, in fact, they are attested only on this inscription.[31] This is not to claim that the men who held them were not wealthy and important, for they certainly were. Only citizens of means could stand for office. Furthermore, selection to one of the nine traditional Archonships conferred membership in the Areopagos, and thus, there existed added attraction in holding them. Importance is a highly relative matter, however; when compared with the offices in Group I, the offices in Group III appear to be relatively minor. This may be illustrated in American terms by contemplating the differences in prestige and importance of a

---

[30]Medeios of Piraeus, Archon in 101/0, is the chief exception. In addition, Xenokles of Rhamnous, ἐπὶ τὰ ἱερά in 103/2, served as Thesmothetes in 100/99; and Aristonymos of Eleusis, General ἐπὶ τὸν Πειραιᾶ about 100 B.C., served as Thesmothetes in 102/1.

[31]Of the 50 known incumbents of the nine Archonships, 31 are unattested elsewhere.

local mayor and town council when set against United States Senators, Representatives, and high cabinet officials. In short, the nine traditional Athenian Archonships, at this time, were stepping-stones to higher office, not the final goal of the politically powerful and ambitious.

The Delian priesthoods in Group IV constitute a special class, distinguished by the fact that they almost never hold secular offices. Of the men recorded on II^2 2336 exceptions are few: Antikrates Epikephisios, Priest of Apollo in 101/0, served as Polemarch in 97/6; Diophantos of Marathon, Priest of the Holy Goddess in 103/2, was ἐπὶ τὰ ἱερά in 99/8. Since both the office of Polemarch and of ἐπὶ τὰ ἱερά had strong connections with the state cults, it may legitimately be questioned whether these are exceptions. Demetrios of Aixone, Priest of Roma in 101/0, also served as Gymnasiarch. Even the one priest who can be identified as belonging to a politically prominent family--namely Demetrios of Anaphlystos--did not himself hold high political office. If a priest is attested as holding more than one office, it is usually another (Delian) priesthood. Furthermore, those whose family connections are known appear to be residents of the Island. The picture thus emerges of a resident clergy devoted to the religious life of the Island and leaving to others the major secular offices.

A DELPHIAN PYTHAIS

The foregoing pages presuppose that the contributions recorded in II^2 2336 were made for the Pythaïs to Delphi. After the appearance of *IG* II^2 2336 in 1931, an edition accompanied by a wealth of prosopographical evidence which emphasized the Delian connections of many of the officials listed, scholars generally accepted Johannes Kirchner's conclusion that the text reflected the foundation of a new Pythaïs to Delos. Dow, in fact, entitled his text "The First Enneëteric Delian Pythaïs, *IG* II^2 2336."

Although the evidence is complicated, the major outlines are clear and leave no doubt that this text refers to Delphi. Some seventy-five years ago Colin in *Le culte d'Apollon pythien à Athènes* (Paris, 1905) pp. 134-139 correctly perceived the general conclusions which could be drawn from the then existing evidence. He concluded on the evidence of *FD* III 2 no. 48, lines 7-8 = *Hesperia* Suppl. 15 p. 60 (which he dated to 97/6, but is now known to belong in 98/7) that sometime prior to 97/6 (i.e. 98/7) the Athenians decided to send the Pythaïs to Delphi at eight-year intervals, instead of at irregular intervals. Pursuant to this decision a Pythaïs was sent in 98/7. Noting the similarity of phrasing between *FD* III 2 no. 54 and the preamble of II^2 2336, he deduced that II^2 2336 referred to the Pythaïs of 98/7 and also saw that ['Αμφικρ]άτης should be restored in line 2.[1]

---

[1]He cited as evidence the references to this man in *FD* III 2 no. 13, line 20 and no. 32, lines 4-5. Kirchner, *IG* II^2 2336 p. 688, and H. Pomtow, *SIG* II^3 pp. 351-352, argued that this restoration was impossible on grounds of spacing; G. Daux, *Delphes au IIe et au Ier siècle* (Paris, 1936) p. 581 n. 1, properly refuted them.

Colin realized that the first eight-year interval should run from 106/5 to 98/7 but could not reconcile to this the dates of II^2 2336 which were then determined as 102/1-94/3 (now firmly established as 103/2-97/6). Ferguson took up the problem and argued that although the limits of the first enneëteris were 102/1 and 95/4 (on the evidence of the then established dates of II^2 2336), the Pythaïs could be dispatched in any year during this interval.[2] While ingenious, this suggestion did not gain many adherents. The discrepancy of the dates remained and, together with the occurrence of the Delian officials on II^2 2336, eventually led first Kirchner (IG II^2 2336), then Ferguson (ATC pp. 147-149 n. 1), Daux (Delphes p. 580), and Dow (HSCP 51, 1940, p. 111ff.), to postulate the foundation of an enneëteric Pythaïs to Delos, not attested anywhere else, overlapping the period of the Delphian enneëteris.[3]

---

[2] Klio 9 (1909) p. 304ff.

[3] The rather exquisite difficulties raised by this theory do not seem to have been considered adequately by its proponents. (1) The confusion of terminology: surely, if two enneëteric Pythaïds had been instituted within three years of one another, we might expect the language of the preamble of II^2 2336 to stipulate to which of the "first" enneëteric Pythaïds it applied. Kirchner perceived this difficulty and restored in line 2 τῆς εἰς Δῆλον πυθαίδος. Dow's publication of frg. y' (EM 12799) revealed that this restoration was incorrect and, furthermore, that nothing in the wording of the preamble pointed to a Delian Pythaïs. (2) The resources required: it appears to have been assumed without question that Athens had the wealth necessary to mount two costly holy processions every eight years. The present study reveals that the Athenian officials, in fact, were rather hard pressed to fund the one procession.

The organization of the text suggests, as has been shown <u>supra</u>, pp. 92-97, that there was an extraordinary fund-raising effort mounted during 98/7 followed by some additional contributions made by the officials of 97/6. The subscriptions on II^2 2336 were, therefore, coordinated with the dispatch of the Pythaïs to Delphi at the end of 98/7. Why do the subscriptions not begin in 106/5 or 105/4, i.e. at the beginning of the interval between the processions? The preamble of II^2 2336 provides some strong clues. It reveals that Amphikrates was authorized, as a result of legislation proposed by Xenotimos of Myrrhinoutta, to publish a list of the Archons who contributed ἀπαρχαί. This legislation was apparently not enacted until 103/2. It had, we may imagine, become clear by then that, if some organized collection effort were not undertaken, the Pythaïs of 98/7 would go to Delphi nearly empty-handed. The original charge to Amphikrates in 106/5 seems, therefore, to have been a vague one of being ὁ ἐπὶ τὰς ἀπαρχάς (<u>FD</u> III 2 no. 13_{20}). When it became clear that this was not sufficient, the legislation of 103/2 put some teeth into the charge by authorizing him to make a public record of the contributions and also by specifying who were to give and how much. Thus, we can account for the dates of the text in an intelligible manner, without resorting to the creation of an otherwise unattested Delian Pythaïs.

The text of <u>FD</u> III 2 no. 54 throws some additional light on the problem. Now known to belong to the Pythaïs of 106/5,[4] it complements <u>FD</u> III 2 no. 6 of the year 98/7, for the one names Amphikrates as ἐπὶ τὴν ἐξαποστολὴν τῆς Πυθαΐδος καὶ τὰς ἀπαρχὰς τοῦ θεοῦ and the other

---

[4]<u>BCH</u> 99 (1975) pp. 195-196.

Sarapion.[5] Together with the evidence of II^2 2336, these two texts reveal that the charge conferred was a complicated one which involved not only the dispatch of the procession with the first fruits, but also supervision during the intervening years of the collection of revenues for the next celebration. Thus, Amphikrates was in charge of the dispatch of the Pythaïs and first fruits of 106/5 and also of collecting moneys for the next celebration in 98/7. Sarapion was in charge in 98/7 and was to direct the collection for the planned Pythaïs in 90/89. The turmoil in the Aegean made the Pythaïs of 98/7 the first and only enneëteric Pythaïs.

In addition to the problem posed by the dates, Kirchner and later Ferguson considered the appearance of so many Delian officials proof that the Pythaïs was one to Delos. Ferguson, for example, wrote (<u>ATC</u> p. 147 n. 1) "The participation of the priests at Delos alone in the collections recorded in <u>IG</u> II^2 2336 is decisive. Had it been the Delphian Pythaïs that was involved the priests at Athens must have contributed." This statement involves a misunderstanding of the nature of those contributing on II^2 2336. The contributors are specifically defined by the preamble as Archons (τοὺς δόντας τῶν ἀρχόντων), i.e. annual officials of the Athenians who were either chosen by lot or elected. The legislation proposed by Xenotimos did indeed single out all of the annual Delian offices (<u>supra</u>, p. 110). This fact merely underlines the importance which the Island had assumed in Athenian affairs by 100 B.C. and does nothing to justify the conclusion that the Pythaïs in question was Delian. Rather, these Delian offices and their incumbents had in general

---

[5]<u>FD</u> III 2 no. 54, lines 3-4, 12 (as re-edited in <u>BCH</u> 99 pp. 195-196); no. 6, lines 2-3, 5; see also the very similar phrasing of II^2 2336, lines 1-2.

achieved sufficient wealth and prominence that they could naturally be tapped for contributions in a time of need.

Furthermore, the Delian officials provide by their absence a small, but very strong, bit of additional evidence revealing the Delphian nature of the Pythaïs. It is a striking feature of II^2 2336 that during the fourth year and after (i.e. for about 60% of the list) the officials who served on Delos, particularly the priests, did not contribute regularly, indeed, hardly at all (see the checklists pp.100-104). It is inconceivable, were the Pythaïs one to Delos, that the priests who served on the Island would, or could, practically speaking, refuse to support their own religious institutions. When, however, the Pythaïs involved is recognized as Delphian, then their refusal becomes a natural unwillingness to enrich at their own expense the rival shrine and/or to be the only priests expected to contribute (supra, p.105).

II^2 2336 then records contributions of ἀπαρχαί for the Pythaïs of 98/7. The fluctuations in contributions, as well as actual interruptions in the subscription, reveal that there were difficulties. In fact, the Pythaïs of 98/7 turned out to be the last of four grand processions sent to Delphi in the latter part of the second century B.C. The others were sent in 138/7, 128/7, and 106/5. All are known to us from the inscriptions commemorating the participants which were engraved on the south wall of the Athenian Treasury at Delphi.[6] The purpose of the celebrations seems to have been to renew old traditions and, by so doing,

---

[6] FD III 2 nos. 2-56 as augmented by S.V. Tracy, "Notes on the Inscriptions of the Pythaïs of 98/7," BCH 93 (1969) pp. 371-395 and "Notes on the Pythaïs Inscriptions," BCH 99 (1975) 185-218. On the texts of 98/7, see also Hesperia Suppl. 15 pp. 48-68.

to reassert the importance of Athens in Greek affairs.[7] It is, for example, significant that the Athenians took this initiative towards Delphi in the year 138/7, less than a decade after the destruction of Corinth. No doubt the growing prosperity resulting from the trade on Delos and the importance of the cult of Apollo on the Island encouraged them. The particular impetus for the sending of the Pythaïds, however, seems to have been an attempt to win the support of Delphi for the Athenian Dionysiac artists in their dispute with the Nemean and Isthmian guilds of Dionysiac artists.[8] It is notable that the Dionysiac artists comprised a large proportion (20-30%) of the participants in all but the first Pythaïs;[9] even in that Pythaïs two of their number organized and directed the chorus honoring Apollo (FD III 2 no. 11_{21-22}). Moreover, the unusually large Pythaïds of 128/7 and 106/5 each followed, the one immediately, the other by a few years, actions taken by the Amphiktyonic Council and by the Roman Senate (with the apparent support of the Amphiktyons) confirming the privileges and primacy of the Athenian guild.[10] These decisions had the effect of proclaiming Athens' cultural

---

[7]On the Pythaïs, see Colin, *Le culte d'Apollon Pythien...*, especially pp. 1-18; A. Boethius, *Die Pythaïs* (Uppsala, 1918); Daux, *Delphes*, pp. 521-583, 708-729.

[8]On this dispute, see in particular G. Klaffenbach, *Symbolae ad Historiam Collegiorum Artificum Bacchiorum* (Berlin, 1914) pp. 24-46; Daux, *Delphes* pp. 356-372; and A.W. Pickard-Cambridge, *The Dramatic Festivals of Athens*, 2nd edition revised by J. Gould and D.M. Lewis (Oxford, 1968), pp. 288-291.

[9]For the statistics, see *BCH* 99 (1975) pp. 215-218.

[10]In 130/29 the Amphiktyons renewed the special privileges granted to the Athenian artists in the early third century B.C. (*FD* III 2 no. 68) and in 112 B.C. the Senate confirmed the primacy of the Athenian guild (*FD* III 2 no. 70, lines 53-66). On the relationship of the Pythaïs of 128/7 to the renewal of privileges in 130/29, see also *Hesperia* 39 (1970) pp. 309-310 and *BCH* 99 (1975) pp. 194-195.

leadership in Greece, especially in the field of drama where she could indeed lay special claim to pre-eminence. The vindication of that claim seems to have been particularly important to the Athenians. Indeed it appears very probable that the important decision to send the Pythaïs on a regular eight-year basis was made in the aftermath of the final settlement of the dispute in Athens' favor in 112 B.C.[11] In short, the Athenian guild seems to have been involved instrumentally in the sending of these grand Pythaïds of the late second century B.C. and the members of the guild comprised a significant portion of the contingent.

The Pythaïs was a special Athenian embassy to Delphi to offer homage to Apollo with sacrifices and games, to present the traditional "first fruits," and to bring the symbolic sacred fire from Delphi to Athens. The procession had many purposes, religious, political, and cultural, as well as conferring the inevitable social and economic advantages of a large panegyris.

> It was an almost pandemic exodus. For three days in going, and as many in returning, men, women, and children, to the number of five hundred or more, were on the road. The distance was over one hundred miles; hence provisions had to be carried, and sleeping-places arranged in advance. First marched the ephebes, sometimes one hundred strong; then the *Pythaïs* proper, made up of *theori*, *pythaistae*, and *canephori*--the elite of the city, under the management of high officials--

---

[11] *BCH* 99 (1975) p. 196.

> who were flanked on either side by the Athenian knights and light-armed cavalry, and attended by a great chorus of flute-players, singers, poets, actors, and all the various gentry who belonged to the gild of Dionysiac artists.[12]

II^2 2336 records a small part of the money involved in the sending of the procession, for it provides a record only of the official ἀπαρχαί or first fruits offered by the city of Athens to Apollo.[13] The other expenses for food, travel, and accommodations were, no doubt, borne by the individual participants and their families or, in the case of Dionysiac artists, by the guild.

---

[12]W.S. Ferguson, Hellenistic Athens (London, 1911) pp. 372-373; see also his remarks in Klio 9 (1909) pp. 307-309.

[13]It seems highly unlikely that ἀπαρχαί could have any other meaning than the technical one of "first fruits" in the phrases ἐπὶ τὴν ἐξαποστολὴν τῆς Πυθαΐδος καὶ τὰς ἀπαρχὰς τοῦ θεοῦ (FD III 2 nos. 6 and 54) and τοὺς δόντας τῶν ἀρχόντων τὰς ἀπαρχὰς τῶι Ἀπόλλωνι τῶι Πυθίωι (II^2 2336, line 3).

II. ATHENS IN 100 B.C.

BACKGROUND: THE ACQUISITION OF DELOS

One of the most significant events for Athens in the second century B.C. was the acquisition of Delos in the political aftermath of the third Macedonian War in 167/6 B.C.[1] The Island became a cleruchy of Athens and was declared a free port. This of course happened as a consequence of actions taken by the Roman Senate. Delos grew rapidly in importance and, following the destruction of Corinth in 146 B.C. and the organization of the province of Asia after 133 B.C., it became the undisputed center of trade in the entire Aegean area. The Athenians who inhabited the Island and governed it thus faced increasingly weighty responsibilities and opportunities. In particular, as Delos grew in commercial importance, a large, non-Athenian, transient, and commercially powerful community grew up on the Island. The Italian part of that community was among the

---

[1]When the research for the present study was largely completed, I was invited in May of 1977 to present a paper,"Athens in 100 B.C.", to the annual meeting of the Association of Ancient Historians in Ottawa. That paper was later revised and published in HSCP 83 (1979) pp. 213-235. The first three paragraphs of this account are taken nearly verbatim from section I of that study. Otherwise, I have tried as much as possible to avoid repetition and refer the reader to it at the appropriate places.

largest and the most influential.[2] It does not require much imagination to contemplate the problems of jurisdiction and the need for firm, effective policies governing trade on the Island.

In the first few years after the Athenian assumption of control, there occurred a dispute between a certain Demetrios of Rhenea, head of the Sarapeion on Delos, and the Athenian officials governing the Island. The details are obscure but the outcome is clear thanks to the discovery of an inscription, ID 1510.[3] Apparently the Athenians moved to close Demetrios' shrine; he appealed, going to Rome himself to present his case before the Senate which acted in his favor. He returned to Athens with a copy of the favorable Senatus Consultum, where there ensued protracted discussion in the Boule, followed by

---

[2]Cf. Ferguson, Hellenistic Athens pp. 346-414; Roussel, DCA pp. 33-96; J. Hatzfeld, Les trafiquants italiens dans l'orient hellénique (Paris, 1919) pp. 30-37; W.A. Laidlaw, A History of Delos (Oxford, 1933) pp. 201-231 and M. Rostovtzeff, The Social and Economic History of the Hellenistic World (Oxford, 1953) pp. 786-799.

[3]Number 5 in R.K. Sherk, Roman Documents from the Greek East (Baltimore, 1969) pp. 37-39.

the issuance of a terse letter from the Athenian Generals to Kharmides, Epimeletes of Delos. The text of the first fourteen lines reads as follows:

οἱ στρατηγοὶ Χαρμίδηι ἐπιμελη|τεῖ Δήλου
χαίρειν· γενομένων| πλειόνων λόγων ἐν
τεῖ βουλεῖ| περὶ τοῦ δόγματος οὗ ἤνεγκεν|
5 ἐκ Ῥώμης Δημήτριος Ῥηναι|εὺς ὑπὲρ τῶν
κατὰ τὸ Σαραπι|εῖον, ἔδοξεν μὴ κωλύειν
αὐ|τὸν ἀνοίγειν καὶ θεραπεύειν|τὸ ἱερὸν καθάπερ
10 καὶ πρότε|ρον· γράψαι δὲ καὶ πρός σε
πε|ρὶ τούτων ἵνα εἰδῇς· ὑποτε|τάχαμεν
δέ σοι καὶ τοῦ ἐνε|χθέντος ὑπ' αὐτοῦ
δόγματος| τὸ ἀντίγραφον.

This is clearly not the language of a decree of the Athenian people. No such decree was ever passed, the reason being that it was not within the competence of the Athenian Boule and assembly to pass on Senatus Consulta. So, after much discussion in the Boule, the generals asserted reality with their laconic letter to the governor. If nothing else, this document makes it clear that the Athenian acquisition of Delos had come on one condition at least, namely the recognition of the ultimate authority of the acts of the Roman Senate with regard to Delos, though it is difficult to imagine that in practice it stopped there. In the two generations which followed, the Athenians clearly recognized the authority of Rome and worked successfully within it, achieving, through their effective administration of the Island, a high degree of prosperity and a renewed prominence for themselves and their city.[4] II^2 2336 provides much of the specific evidence for this reconstruction.

The years immediately following the period covered by II^2 2336 brought the necessity for _de facto_ alliance with one of the principals in the conflict between Rome and Mithridates for control of the Aegean. At this juncture, ca. 90 B.C., the Island and the mother city apparently went different ways; Athens supported Mithridates, Delos Rome. The inscription thus sheds welcome light on Athens in the years just prior to the Mithridatic War and the Sullan destruction, an important turning point in the history of the city.[5]

---

[4]For an assessment of the economic situation, see J. Day, _An Economic History of Athens under Roman Domination_ (New York, 1942) pp. 50-119.

[5]On the political situation in Athens leading up to this war, see E. Badian, "Rome, Athens, and Mithridates," _AJAH_ 1 (1976) pp. 105-128.

DELIAN CONNECTIONS

Several individuals and families were prominent in Athenian public life during the years 103/2 to 97/6.[1] The families headed by Sarapion of Melite, Medeios of Piraeus, Pyrrhos of Lamptrai, Hestiaios and Theokharis of the Kerameikos, Aristion of Oion, and Ammonios of Anaphlystos dominate. The litany of their officeholding in these years is impressive:

103/2 Ammonios held the Hoplite Generalship.

102/1 Sarapion was Hoplite General.

101/0 Medeios held the Eponymous Archonship; Theokharis served as Herald of the Areopagos; Aristion was Epimeletes of Emporion; Hestiaios was Agoranomos on Delos.

100/99 Hestiaios served as Hoplite General; Sarapion was Epimeletes of Delos; Medeios directed the Public Bank on Delos (supra, p. 94 n. 14).

99/8 Medeios held the Hoplite Generalship; Pyrrhos directed the Public Bank on Delos; Theokharis served as ὁ ἐπὶ τὰ ἱερά.

98/7 Sarapion was Hoplite General; Pyrrhos served as Herald of the Areopagos; Medeios acted as Epimeletes of Delos.

---

[1]Prominence is defined as holding one or more of the offices in Group I. See supra, pp. 112, 144f. and the discussion there for the justification of this. For a full treatment of each of the individuals discussed in this section, see the prosopographical index.

97/6 Pyrrhos held the Hoplite Generalship; Aristion served as Epimeletes of Delos.

Sarapion, Medeios, and Pyrrhos were clearly the most influential men in Athens during the years represented by II^2 2336.[2] During this seven year period, each held three of the offices in Group I; no other individual held an equal number during these years. In addition, Sarapion and Medeios each gave an extraordinarily large sum of money to finance the Pythaïs.[3] The evidence indeed suggests that the two men used their consecutive terms as Hoplite General in 99/8 and 98/7 to take the lead in organizing a concerted last-minute

---

[2]Diodoros son of Theophilos of Halai (PA 3935, stemma in NPA p. 56) is also assigned an important role by Ferguson, Hellenistic Athens pp. 421, 426, and 429, and by C. Mossé, Athens in Decline 404-86 B.C. (London, 1973) p. 143, following Ferguson. In fact he served as Epimeletes of Piraeus Harbor in 112/1 (II^2 1012) and supervised the repair of weights and measures about the same time (II^2 1013, line 39). He was also active in the Pythaïs of 98/7, participating himself as a pythaïst (FD III 2 nos. 31 and 17, line 24 = Hesperia Suppl. 15 p. 54) and was accompanied by his three sons Theophilos, Philanthes, and Diopeithes, who acted as theoroi of Kekropis (FD III 2 nos. 10 and 2, lines 33-35 = Hesperia Suppl. 15 p. 50). A number of descendants are known (II^2 1961, line 3; II^2 2877; II^2 2464, lines 3-4; Trans. Am. Philosoph. Soc. 64, 1974, p. 51, line 7). His importance seems somewhat exaggerated by Ferguson, for he is not attested as holding any of the major offices, nor is he known on Delos, or from II^2 2336.

[3]Over the entire seven years, Sarapion contributed 1550 drachmas and Medeios 1200.

effort to raise the funds needed to support the Pythaïs.[4] Cooperation between them seems probable and is likely on other grounds. For example, they served together on Delos in 100/99. The fact that Sarapion held the Hoplite Generalship twice suggests that he was the senior of the two men.[5] Indeed it can hardly be an accident that Sarapion was elected to the office in 98/7 and thus *ex officio* headed the Pythaïs to Delphi.[6]

In addition to their political cooperation, it appears probable that there was a fruitful marriage connection between Sarapion and Medeios. Medeios had a sister Philippa (*ID* 1869). Pseudo-Plutarch (*Decem Oratorum Vitae* 843 B), in a list of descendants of Lykourgos, much of which can be checked against inscriptions and can be shown to be highly accurate,[7] informs us that Διοκλῆς ὁ Μελιτεύς married

---

[4]*Supra*, pp. 93-97 and *HSCP* 83 (1979) pp. 224-225.

[5]Medeios was a child pythaïst, say 12 years of age, in 128/7; thus in 98/7 he was about 42 years old. Sarapion could have been as many as 20 years his senior. On the relationship between them, see also *HSCP* 83 (1979) p. 227.

[6]In view of the large amount of money which Medeios contributed for the Pythaïs, it is surprising that he did not participate in it. He did not--at least the inscriptions from Delphi (the record is virtually complete) do not list him or any member of his family. Note, however, that Sundwall (*NPA* p. 116) restored as one of the kanephoroi of 106/5 the name of Laodamia sister of Medeios in line 8 of *FD* III 2 no. 30 = Daux, *Delphes*, p. 713. The restoration seems arbitrary.

[7]See the references *ad loc.* in J. Mau, *Plutarchi Moralia* V. 2.1 (B.G. Teubner, 1971); also *ID* 1869 and *Trans.Am. Philosoph. Soc.* 64 (1974) p. 51, lines 21-22.

Philippa the sister of Medeios. This man is not with certainty attested elsewhere. He is likely, however, to have belonged to a prominent family from Melite. The nomen Diokles is well attested in Sarapion of Melite's family--one of his sons and several of his descendants bore it.[8] Given the prominence of Sarapion and his family, it appears very likely that the man who married Medeios' sister was a close relative of Sarapion, either his son or, perhaps, a cousin.

In addition to the probable connection with Sarapion's family, Medeios enjoyed through his mother, Timothea, who was the daughter of Glaukos of the Piraeus,[9] a longstanding connection with that influential family, two members of which, Diogenes and Aropos, served as Epimeletes of Delos, one in 115/4 and the other in 94/3.[10] The latter was honored with a statue set up by the Greeks, the Romans, and the Athenians on the Island, and was especially praised in an epigram carved on the base for safeguarding the decisions of the Romans.[11]

Another old family with which Medeios had distant ties was that of Kallias son of Habron of Bate, a family which also could claim a relationship to the orator Lykourgos.[12] Members of this family took

---

[8] ID 2364; Trans. Am. Philosoph. Soc. 64 (1974) p. 51, line 22.

[9] Decem Oratorum Vitae 843B; ID 1869.

[10] On Diogenes (PA 3844), who also served as Director of the Public Bank, see ID 1839 and 1670; and on Aropos (PA 2248), ID 1658 and 1763; see stemmata in PA II p. 82 and NPA p. 54.

[11] ID 1658, lines 10-11.

[12] See the stemma in PA I p. 2 and Decem Oratorum Vitae 842F-843A.

part in the Pythaïds of 128/7, 106/5, and 98/7 serving as ἐξηγηταί and representing the Genos of the Eupatrids.[13] No members of the family are attested on II^2 2336. One, however, Δράκων 'Οφέλου Βατῆθεν, served as Epimeletes of Delos in 112/1.[14] Another probable member of this family, Hediste daughter of Habron, married Diokles of Melite, the son of Medeios' sister Philippa.[15] Thus, it seems clear that the ties of these families were renewed and made closer during Medeios' lifetime. In short, Sarapion and Medeios were not only very powerful men, but also sought to augment their family fortunes through advantageous marriage alliances.

Nothing has come down to us concerning Sarapion's origin; this probably means nothing more than that our evidence is deficient and not, as one scholar has recently claimed, that he was an upstart.[16] What, after all, would we know about Medeios' origins, if it were not for the genealogy given in Pseudo-Plutarch? Almost nothing. Sarapion is attested on Delos just thrice (ID 1870, 2005, and 2364); perhaps these attestations all belong to the year 100/99, when he served as Epimeletes of the Island. Medeios on the other hand was most probably a resident of the Island, for he was honored there by his parents as a

---

[13]FD III 2 nos. 24, line 9; 13, line 4; 5, line 19; and 6, line 13.

[14]ID 1653, 2614, 2229. Otherwise the charges known to be fulfilled by this family were primarily religious in nature (J. Oliver, The Athenian Expounders of the Sacred and Ancestral Law, Baltimore, 1950, p. 143).

[15]Decem Oratorum Vitae 843 B; see the stemma in PA II p. 82.

[16]P. MacKendrick, The Athenian Aristocracy 399-31 B.C. (Cambridge, 1969) p. 55.

Deliastes (ID 1869) in ca. 115 B.C. and served as trierarch on the Island (ID 1841).[17] His father was ἐξηγητής of the Eumolpids and Medeios himself held the Priesthood of Poseidon-Erechtheus.[18] Sarapion disappears from the record after 98/7; but members of his family survived the turbulent years into the post-Sullan period. One probable descendant served as Hoplite General[19] and others are known in a decree of the Κήρυκες of 20/19.[20]

Medeios remained active as the head of those who favored a policy of supporting Rome during the years around 90 B.C. He held illegally, and thus probably as a dictator of sorts, the Archonship for a continuous three year period from 91/0 to 89/8 (II^2 1713_{9-11}). When the pro-Mithridatic elements gained the ascendancy, he was no doubt forced to flee. It was during the period from late 88 to early 86 that his name suffered damnatio memoriae on II^2 2336, lines 183-189.[21] It was soon re-inscribed and the family continued in influence in the years after 86. His son held the Archonship in ca. 65 B.C. (II^2 1095, 2874) and also served as ἐξηγητής of the Eumolpids (II^2 3490).

---

[17]The name Μήδειος, without patronymic or demotic, coupled with the name Θεόδοτος, also without patronymic or demotic, is prominent among graffiti found on Delos; BCH 13 (1889) pp. 374-376 and pl. XIII and BCH 29 (1905) pp. 248-250. Ferguson (Hellenistic Athens p. 421) suggests that they are Medeios of Piraeus and Theodotos of Sounion; it would be nice, but there is no proof.

[18]Decem Oratorum Vitae 843 B.

[19]Ibid.

[20]Trans. Am. Philosoph. Soc. 64 (1974) p. 51, lines 21-22.

[21]Commentary ad loc.

As illustrious as Sarapion and Medeios was Pyrrhos of Lamptrai, who is known during his career to have held four of the offices in Group I. In addition to being Director of the Public Bank on Delos (99/8?), Hoplite General (97/6), and Herald of the Areopagos (98/7), he served as Epimeletes of Delos in 104/3 (ID 2599). His brother Buttakos, known from II^2 2336 as Epimeletes of Piraeus in 102/1, served as Gymnasiarch on Delos in 104/3 (ID 2599). The family is attested on the Island in the previous two generations as well, their grandfather being Epimeletes in 153/2 (ID 1432 Aa I_3) and their uncle serving as ἐπὶ τὰ ἱερά in ca. 135 (ID 2041). Pyrrhos had at least two children, a daughter Anthe, who was honored as an ergastina in 108/7[22] and a son Buttakos who participated as a child pythaïst in the Pythaïs of 98/7.[23] Only one member of the family is known after 97/6.[24]

Hestiaios from the Kerameikos (Hoplite General in 100/99, Agoranomos in 101/0) and his cousin Theokharis (Herald of the Areopagos in 101/0, ἐπὶ τὰ ἱερά in 99/8), Aristion son of Sokrates of Oion (Epimeletes of Emporion in 101/0, Epimeletes of Delos in 97/6), and Ammonios of Anaphlystos (Hoplite General in 103/2) also stand out in the record which II^2 2336 affords us. In addition to the offices recorded on II^2 2336, Theokharis is known as Kosmetes of the Athenian

---

[22] II^2 1036 as re-published by C.A. Hutton in BSA 24 (1914-1916) p. 159, line 32.

[23] FD III 2 no. 17 = Hesperia Suppl. 15 p. 54, line 58. See also BCH 93 (1969) p. 381.

[24] II^2 6663, dated near the end of the 1st century B.C.

ephebic corps in 119/8 (II^2 1008_{46}); the family is not otherwise known in Athens or on Delos. Aristion's father served as Epimeletes of Delos in 117/6 (ID 2055_{19-21}) and is also attested on the Island in a list of distinguished persons.[25] The family is not known subsequent to 97/6. Ammonios himself was Epimeletes of Delos in 107/6 (ID 2232). He comes from a family with longstanding Delian connections; at least three other members served as Epimeletes of the Island.[26]

Other individuals prominent on II^2 2336 are Theodotos son of Diodoros of Sounion (Epimeletes of Delos in 102/1); Polykleitos son of Alexander of Phlya (Epimeletes of Delos in 99/8); Andreas son of Andreas from the Piraeus (Herald of the Council of the Areopagos in 97/6); and Arkhias son of Diogenes of Anaphlystos (Epimeletes of Emporion in 99/8, Nauarch probably in 101/0). The Delian connections of these men are notable. Theodotos was priest on Delos in ca. 113/2 and again in 110/9.[27] Polykleitos' son became Epimeletes of the Island (ID 1662). Andreas is known on Delos as early as 119/8 as a frequenter of the gymnasia (ID 2598_{54}) and later became Epimeletes of the Island (ID 2266_7).

In summary the Delian connections of the most prominent men

---

[25] ID 2630, line 3. Lest it be imagined that he resided permanently on Delos, note that he spent much of the year 118/7 in Athens, for he proposed three decrees in that year, one in honor of prytaneis in the month of Maimakterion (Agora XV 253, line 6) and two in honor of ephebes, one in Boedromion, the other in Elaphebolion (II^2 1008, lines 4, 52).

[26] ID 2044, 2125, 2600; see the stemma in Roussel, DCA p. 104.

[27] ID 2261, 2228 with 2626.

appearing on II^2 2336 are very notable. Families great and powerful in the years 103/2 and following had been active on Delos.[28] A consideration of the fortunes of the extremely influential family of Mikion and Eurykleides of Kephisia renders even clearer the important role which Delos played in the last half of the 2nd century B.C. The most powerful and influential members of this family flourished from 230/29 on to ca. 200 B.C.[29] The _floruit_ of Mikion IV (_PA_ 10187), the last truly prominent member of this family, is placed about 163 B.C. He is known from inscriptions on Delos belonging to the early years of the cleruchy as a dedicator of objects in the temple inventories (_ID_ 1403 Bb I_{26}; 1432 Ab I_{30}; Bb II_{8}). No other member of the family is known on Delos after him, though members do appear in Athens as late as 108/7.[30] What happened? Their inland deme and the inland orientation of their building program[31] suggest that they were a landed family of the Mesogaia. Perhaps a commercial life of the kind offered by Delos had no appeal for them. In any case, by the time of II^2 2336, they have been eclipsed by commercial families which have been active on Delos.

The crucial influence of the Island is clear. The men who were politically most influential in Athens in the latter part of the second century B.C. were men from families which had, in most cases it

---

[28]See also _HSCP_ 83 (1979) pp. 217-220.

[29]_PA_ 5966 and the stemma; on them in general, see Ferguson, _Hellenistic Athens_ pp. 205-277.

[30]II^2 1036, line 34 = _BSA_ 21 (1914-16) p. 159.

[31]Ferguson, _Hellenistic Athens_ pp. 237-239.

seems probable, extensive commercial interests on Delos. The leading Athenian families in these years should be considered Delian, in the sense that they resided for extended periods on Delos, made their money in the commercial activities there, and got their initial political experience there. It may legitimately be concluded that Delian businessmen and bankers, men therefore of comparatively broad international experience, were prominent in guiding Athens in its last two generations of vigorous prosperity (146-86 B.C.). This came about as a natural consequence of two factors. First, II^2 2336 reflects a system of government in which people paid for the privilege of holding office instead of being paid. It required considerable means to be able to stand for the highest offices and to meet the financial obligations which they entailed, if one were elected. Wealth, then, may go a long way towards accounting for the Delian connections of the men holding these offices. The commerce on Delos was, after all, the primary source of wealth in this period. Second, the Island was an important international center, the administration of which required business acumen combined with the ability to deal effectively on a daily basis with traders from all over the Mediterranean world.[32] Naturally, men who grew up on the Island and whose families dealt with the international trading community on a regular basis were best qualified for many of the key political and administrative posts.

---

[32]For the breadth of trade on the Island, see especially Rostovtzeff, The Social and Economic History pp. 794-798.

"BETWEEN ROME AND PONTUS"

In 1911 William Scott Ferguson, then an Assistant Professor of History at Harvard University, published his masterful study, Hellenistic Athens, still the standard work. In his final chapter, "Athens between Rome and Pontus," he provided a persuasive account of the political situation in Athens which led up to the Mithridatic wars. A brief summary will be helpful. A commercial aristocracy, based in the trading community on Delos, came into being in the years after 130 B.C. Led by Medeios of the Piraeus, Sarapion of Melite, Theodotos of Sounion, and Diodoros of Halai,[1] these aristocrats, who had been agitating for the removal of certain legal restrictions, such as the need for a judicial audit, overthrew the government in or about the year 103/2. In this they were aided by an adventitious slave revolt. The new aristocratic government subordinated the interests of the average Athenian to the wishes of Rome and to the commercial interests of the trading community on Delos. When, therefore, Mithridates began to challenge the Romans in Asia Minor, naturally the oppressed commons in Athens were sympathetic to his cause and sent an ambassador to him, Athenion, a prominent Peripatetic philosopher. With the support of Mithridates, the commons subsequently elected Athenion Hoplite General and drove out the aristocrats, whom Sulla then reinstated after his bloody victory. Such in bare outline is Ferguson's account.

---

[1]His importance has been exaggerated; p. 160 n. 2 *supra*.

Logical and neat, based on a mass of specific evidence, this reconstruction has prevailed for two generations. While new evidence, especially the fundamental contributions of the great French scholar, Pierre Roussel, to the history of Delos,[2] has tended to corroborate Ferguson's picture of the great extent of Delian influence over Athens in this period, other parts of his reconstruction have not fared so well, in particular the crucial theory of an oligarchic revolution in 103/2, for which today there is no positive evidence whatsoever.[3] In justice to Ferguson, he himself--and this has been neglected by too many students of the period--later realized that the evidence could not sustain the revolution which he had postulated and modified his account to a series of crises, each one of which added to the power of the aristocratic party.[4]

Although we now have more evidence than was available to Ferguson, the basic facts have not changed greatly. What is needed, as Badian has recently pointed out,[5] is a new framework for these facts. Ferguson, and many other historians of the late nineteenth and early twentieth centuries, tended to see events in terms of class

---

[2] DCA, ID.

[3] See Badian, "Rome, Athens...," AJAH 1 (1976) pp. 105-106; Tracy, HSCP 83 (1979) pp. 220-225.

[4] ATC pp. 147-155. On the lack of a judicial audit in II^2 1028, which remained one of Ferguson's cardinal pieces of evidence for the constitutional crises, the present writer (Hesperia Suppl. 15 p. 44 concerning line 118 of II^2 1028) has pointed out that the omission of the formula containing the audit was caused simply by lack of space and not by anything so portentous as a crisis in government.

[5] "Rome, Athens...," AJAH 1 (1976) p. 105ff.

structure, oligarchs versus the commons, tories versus democrats, etc. There is inevitably some truth in views of this kind. Unfortunately the only extensive evidence we have relates to the men who held public office. About all the others we know, and can infer, tantalizingly little. It is necessary, therefore, to concentrate our interpretative energies on the evidence we do have, primarily, in this instance, II^2 2336.

The inscription reveals a very large number of persons of diverse backgrounds holding office year after year. It shows no anomalies in the constitutional process; instead sortition, tribal rotation, the limitation on repeated tenure of Archonships, the prohibition against simultaneous office holding are all very much in evidence.[6] In short, the government was working as well as it ever had. The relative prominence of the men who served as Herald of the Council of the Areopagos does indeed suggest that the Areopagos itself had gained in influence some years prior to 103/2 (<u>supra</u>, pp. 116-117). A logical date would be approximately 130 B.C., i.e. at a time when the growing prosperity from the port on Delos began to be felt in Athens. As the individuals holding public office, who were, as a result of the developed use of the liturgical system, necessarily persons of relatively great means[7]--as these people and the city itself gained

---

[6]See Tables 1-3 pp. 134-135, 142-143 and <u>HSCP</u> 83 (1979) pp. 220-225.

[7]See J.K. Davies, <u>Athenian Propertied Families</u> (Oxford, 1971) pp. xx-xxxi. Though Davies treats the period 600-300 B.C., much of the evidence which he adduces of wealth conferring political power is clearly applicable to later periods as well. "Incontestably, and formal political equality notwithstanding, the influence wielded on public affairs in classical Athens by the deployment of personal wealth--in a word, property-power--cannot at any time be dismissed as negligible" (p. xviii).

added wealth, power, and prestige from their activity in the international trading community on Delos, the Areopagos, whose membership consisted of those who could afford to stand for the nine traditional Archonships, naturally gained in influence. It is also probable that membership in the Areopagos had itself become in practice a prerequisite to holding the highest elective offices, which also must have contributed to the prestige of the body.[8] Good fortune provides us with some important evidence for the year 128/7. In the record of the Pythaïs for that year, the Herald appears in a position of prominence for the first time.[9] It is possible, though scarcely necessary, to imagine the Roman Senate as a model of sorts. The changes which occurred were, it appears, gradual and natural. There are no indications of revolution, constitutional crises, or even struggles between rival groups, though these latter must have existed to some degree.

It cannot be denied that some Athenians grew very wealthy as a result of the commerce on Delos. It is hardly proper, however, to

---

[8] _Supra_, p. 115 and _HSCP_ 83 (1979) pp. 227-229.

[9] _FD_ III 2 no. 3, col. II, lines 3-7 (see the discussion of these lines in _BCH_ 99 [1975] p. 189 n. 14). In addition, the incumbent Μνασικλῆς Μνασικλέους may well (the name is not a common one) be identical with _PA_ 10235, third mint magistrate of ca. 140 B.C. (Thompson, _NSSCA_ p. 575, who dates the coinage to 166/5).

imagine a small aristocracy insensitive to the well-being of the masses.[10] The prosopographical evidence, fragmentary though it is, is extensive, more extensive perhaps than for any other comparable period in Athenian history.[11] II^2 2336 reveals that a large number of persons had the means to stand for office. Nor do they appear to be a closed group. Those we know a good deal about reveal a surprising variety. Men of old families, men of comparatively new ones, unknowns, Athenians with no Delian connections, those who doubtless called Delos home, poets, priests, business men, bankers, all appear.[12] And it should not be forgotten, those who appear

---

[10] As implied e.g. by Ferguson, Hellenistic Athens p. 427: "Hence we shall probably not err in making concern for the maintenance of cordial relations between Athens and Rome--the Rome of Marius and the financial imperialists--the leading motive in the agitation begun by Medeius and his associates."

[11] In addition to II^2 2336, the complete records of the Pythaïds of 128/7, 106/5, and 98/7 survive, which had respectively about 300, 500, and 300 participants known to us by name. Moreover, from Athens itself come well preserved lists of ephebes for the years 128/7 (Hesperia 24, 1955, pp. 220-239), 123/2 (II^2 1006), 119/8 (II^2 1008), 117/6 (II^2 1009), 107/6 (II^2 1011), 102/1 (II^2 1028 = Hesperia Suppl. 15 pp. 32-48); these supply the names of another 524 Athenians. Lastly, the excavations on Delos have brought to light a reasonably long series of inscriptions covering the same period.

[12] For details, see the prosopographical index, particularly the entries for Medeios of the Piraeus, Sarapion of Melite, Skamandrios of Aphidna, Lakrateides of Ikarion, Demetrios of Anaphlystos, Glaukias of Krioa, Buttakos of Lamptrai, and Kharias of Aithalidai.

on II^2 2336 comprised only a small percentage of the total number of officials; there were many other officials for the city, and for each deme, genos, and religious organization.[13]

The strong Delian element in Athenian government at this period, which has led some to postulate a moneyed aristocracy with little concern for the welfare of the city, should instead be seen as a natural consequence of the prosperity which resulted from the administration of the Island. Indeed, if Delian connections were not prominent in many of the most influential families, one would be led to suspect that the importance of the Island for Athens in this period had been exaggerated. In fact, the Island and the wealth accruing from the activity of the free port on it were crucial for Athens; this is reflected clearly in the careers of the men who held office and in the relative importance of the various offices.[14] It is all exactly what we should expect and constitutes no evidence for imagining a divorce between the interests of the city and those of the Island.

At the same time, the inscription does provide some indication of the problems which afflicted the Athenians in this period. Most obviously, they seem to have overestimated their own prosperity. The

---

[13]The most succinct account of these many offices may be found in Ferguson, Hellenistic Athens pp. 471-476. See also Hansen, "Seven Hundred Archai...," GRBS 21 (1980) pp. 151-173.

[14]The proportion of offices on II^2 2336 also seems significant; 14 officials are listed for the city (including Piraeus) and 17 for Delos.

best evidence of this is that provided by the Pythaïds, which may be summarized as follows. Sometime about 110 B.C., the Athenians decided to send the Pythaïs to Delphi on a regular eight-year basis. Their purpose, it appears, was to reciprocate the friendly actions taken by Delphi and the Roman Senate in 112 towards their Dionysiac artists, i.e. towards their cultural heritage of which they were justly proud.[15] The first regular Pythaïs was dispatched to Delphi in 106/5, the second (the first regular enneëteric Pythaïs) was scheduled for 98/7. The economic difficulties involved in mounting this second Pythaïs are obvious from the very need for the existence of II^2 2336.[16] Athenian prosperity had probably begun to decline slowly in the years after 110 as the importance of Puteoli grew[17] and as the Romans began to suppress the slave trade.[18] The revolt of the slaves about 100 B.C. no doubt worsened matters.[19] For the extent of the decline we have little evidence. In any case, the difficulty of raising money for the Pythaïs can hardly be traced to a lack of enthusiasm for it. The evidence here seems clear. Unusually prominent persons sought the Archonships of 98/7; Sarapion himself led

---

[15]*Supra*, pp. 150-153 and *BCH* 99 (1975) pp. 194-196.

[16]*Supra*, p. 148 and *HSCP* 83 (1979) pp. 225-226.

[17]The poet Lucilius as early as ca. 115 B.C. referred to Puteoli as *Delumque minorem* (Marx frg. 123). On the growth of trade in Puteoli, see Day, *An Economic History* p. 118 and Rostovtzeff, *The Social and Economic History* pp. 864 and 959.

[18]Rostovtzeff, *Ibid*. p. 786 and Day, *Ibid*. pp. 117-118. Delos was a major center for the slave trade.

[19]On the revolt, see *HSCP* pp. 232-234.

the procession (supra, pp. 93,134). The inscriptions on the south wall of the Athenian Treasury at Delphi reveal that whole families took part[20] in what must have been a highly festive atmosphere.[21]

II[2] 2336 also provides evidence of internal conflicts and differences of interest in the Athenian political scene. The creation wholesale of a significant number of annual offices for the island of Delos in 167/6 must have created problems, particularly of integrating them into the existing political system. The integration can never have worked fully because of the physical distance and special circumstances of administering an island for an international community, a community which itself did not help matters by more and more taking decisions on its own, independent of Athens and its officials.[22] The nearly complete lack of contributions from Delian officials in the fourth year and only sporadic participation in later years may well reflect in part this unusual situation.[23]

---

[20]See, for example, in the prosopographical index, the evidence concerning Sarapion of Melite and Buttakos and Pyrrhos of Lamptrai. They do not seem to be exceptional; brothers, cousins, fathers and sons appear frequently in the Pythaïs inscriptions (FD III 2 index).

[21]Daux, Delphes p. 561, followed by Day, An Economic History pp. 95 and 117, interprets the smaller size of the Pythaïs of 98/7 as a decline reflecting the political crises in Athens at this time. This is rather too simple. The Pythaïs of 98/7 had nearly 300 participants, i.e. nearly the same number as that of 128/7 which had about 15 more (see BCH 99, 1975, pp. 215-218 for the numbers). It seems more accurate to interpret the Pythaïs of 106/5 as extraordinarily grand (it had over 500 participants) rather than to see that of 98/7 as reflecting a decline.

[22]Roussel, DCA pp. 50-55 and Ferguson, Hellenistic Athens pp. 380-384.

[23]See pp.149-150 for another possible motive.

In addition to this, and of more fundamental importance, the careers of the individuals recorded on II^2 2336 do indicate a separation between offices of greater and lesser importance. The Hoplite General and Epimeletes of Delos are clearly more important than most of the other offices. The truly important offices, those in Groups I and II (<u>supra</u>, pp.113-128,144), are held by men who are generally attested elsewhere and very often in the Delian evidence.[24] They are clearly the most powerful men of the time. The offices of Group III (<u>supra</u>, pp.129-134,144), the traditional Archonships of the mother city, are not usually held by men equally prominent in our evidence. The important question to consider is what this indicates about the political relationship between Athens and Delos, if anything. It would be possible for one to suppose, following Ferguson's lead, that the important offices and men are largely Delian and, therefore, that Delian interests are unduly controlling Athens in this period. But is this in fact the best way to interpret II^2 2336? I think not. The inscription provides us with a very valuable cross section of Athenian government for seven consecutive years. But that is all it provides. As for the make-up of the government in the generation before and after, we are largely in the dark, for names of officeholders have not come down to us in significant numbers. A certain amount of speculation is therefore necessary.

---

[24]See also <u>HSCP</u> 83 (1979) pp. 216-220.

The offices in Group III, that is, the nine traditional Archonships, seemed to have appealed to two distinct types of individuals: namely, politically ambitious men on the way up and more senior men with little political ambition who enjoyed the prestige of the office. It appears probable that these Archonships were largely ceremonial; there were, to be sure, daily duties, probably of a routine nature, attached to them and, above all, financial obligations entailed in them. In return, however, holding one of them conferred membership in the increasingly prestigious Council of the Areopagos. Thus, these offices were sought by the politically ambitious individual early in his career as a natural stepping stone on the way to higher office. We may safely assume, therefore, that most of the officials recorded in II^2 2336 as holding the offices in Groups I and II were senior officials who had held one of the nine traditional Archonships at an earlier point in their careers, the record of which has not survived to us.[25] This accounts in a plausible manner for why so few of the men in Groups I and II are known, in our evidence, to have held a traditional Archonship. And the men who are listed on II^2 2336 as holding the traditional Archonships and who are generally unknown otherwise may be assumed either to be relatively young men moving up in politics, men whose careers were affected

---

[25]Medeios appears to be exceptional in holding the Eponymous Archonship and the major offices so close together in time. But, we should not forget that he was ca. 40 years old when he was Archon and that his political career was, by any standard, meteoric (HSCP 83, 1979, p. 227).

adversely by the Mithridatic War and the Sullan depredations, or senior men who were not greatly active in public life but who enjoyed the honor conferred by occasional public service.

Despite the very real indications from II^2 2336 of disruptions of financial problems, of unwillingness to contribute, and of general differences in status of offices and individuals, there is nothing to warrant seeing some sort of split between the mercantile interests in Delos/Athens on the one hand and the average citizens in the city on the other. Good sense in fact says otherwise. Medeios, Sarapion, and Pyrrhos, elected frequently to the most important posts by the Athenians, can scarcely have ignored the interests of the Athenians and still have been elected. At the same time, they must have harbored few illusions about the Romans and their military/economic power. Their policy was undoubtedly one of careful accommodation of the Romans and Italians, especially the trading interests on Delos, while doing what was possible to preserve and further Athenian interests.[26] There is no reason to believe that the people were not behind them, though there may well have been lack of agreement on just how far to pursue this policy. No doubt those with extensive commercial interests saw the need for accommodation more acutely and were willing to pursue such a policy farther than those without such interests. Still, the evidence suggests that nearly every Athenian

---

[26]See E. Gruen's sensible article on the attitude of the Rhodians towards Rome in the third Macedonian war ("Rome and Rhodes in the Second Century B.C.," CQ 69, 1975, pp. 58-81, esp. p. 70ff.). The Greeks seem to have been wily, though often helpless, political realists.

shared to some extent in the prosperity created by the port on Delos[27] and concurred to some degree with a policy of cooperation, if not outright accommodation.

The misfortune of Athens and her leaders was to be completely at the mercy of Roman power. The threat posed by Mithridates eventually forced Rome's hand. No doubt there were appeals to Rome by various groups in Athens. In the crisis, Rome demanded absolute obedience from those who led Athens and imposed the illegal triple Archonship of Medeios in 91-88[28] as an interim measure until Mithridates had been dealt with. This was going too far and drove many persons, including even, we may imagine, some with extensive commercial interests, to temporize or to oppose Rome outright.[29] In either case, the result was inevitable.

In conclusion, this study has concentrated on one important Athenian inscription and through it upon Athens, its citizens, and, so far as possible, its institutions. There exists some danger of forgetting that Athens at this time played out a relatively small role on a very large stage. It was caught up in the expansion of Rome into one of the first true world powers. In contrast, Athens by the end of the third century B.C. had lost all but the memory of its greatness.

---

[27]On Athens' prosperity in the years 138 to 100, see <u>HSCP</u> 83 (1979) pp. 229-231.

[28]For a slightly different account, cf. Badian, "Rome, Athens,...," <u>AJAH</u> 1 (1976) p. 108. It is impossible for Medeios to have held the triple Archonship without the blessing of Rome.

[29]<u>Ibid</u>. pp. 112-114. For the names of aristocrats caught in the middle, see II[2] 1714 with Badian's note 30 on p. 124.

It owed, as both its leaders and citizens clearly recognized, its prosperity and central position in the Aegean directly to the action of the Roman Senate after Pydna.[30] What the Romans had given, they could take away, if it suited their purposes, as they had in the case of Rhodes.[31] The Athenian leaders of necessity were playing a delicate and, as some of them must have realized, dangerous game. At the same time, as Athens became more prosperous, its position in the eyes of the Romans became more sensitive. The city, which in 167 had been so weak that it seemed a safe transit port, possessing neither the naval strength of Rhodes nor the political power of Corinth, had, by 100 B.C., become a significant link in the economy of the East.[32] Thus, the Roman insistence on the loyalty of Athens during the crisis and the harsh treatment for seeming disobedience.

---

[30]The significant mention which the Romans receive in decrees of ca. 100 B.C. from Delphi, Athens, and Delos makes this clear. See e.g. FD III 2 no. 48, line 7; no. 68, lines 60-61 = II^2 1132, line 94; II^2 1028, line 15; the recurrent phrase in prytany decrees after ca. 200 B.C., ἐφ' ὑγιείαι καὶ σωτηρίαι τῆς βουλῆς καὶ τοῦ δήμου καὶ τῶν συμμάχων, refers to the Romans in part as Dow has suggested (Hesperia Suppl. 1 pp. 9-10); ID 2252, lines 3-4; 1642, lines 1-2; 1643, lines 1-2. In this connection, the celebration of the Romaia at Athens in 148/7 (II^2 1938) and the very existence of the Priest of Roma on II^2 2336 provide eloquent testimony of the extent of Roman influence over the Athenians. See further Mellor, ΘΕΑ ΡΩΜΗ, Hypomnemata 42.

[31]Concerning Rome's arbitrary treatment of Rhodes, see Gruen, "Rome and Rhodes...," CQ 69 (1975) p. 79ff.

[32]Day, An Economic History pp. 60-61.

In the final analysis, it is sobering to reflect how little the actions of the individual Athenians recorded on this inscription really mattered when the crisis came. Their Indian summer,[33] however real, was short-lived and dependent on factors beyond their control.

---

[33] The phrase is MacKendrick's (Athenian Aristocracy, p. 55).

III. INDICES

PROSOPOGRAPHICAL INDEX

Please note that the partially preserved names in lines 9, 27, 66, 68, 72, 76, 171, 216, 221, 236 are not included in this index, for nothing could be said about them beyond repeating the text.

In compiling this index, the following sources have been used: PA; NPA; Hesperia Index 1-10, Suppl. 1-6; 11-20, Suppl. 7-9; and the separate indices of Hesperia vols. 21-49, of Ath. Mitt. 67 (1942), of FD III 2, of Agora XV, and of Agora XVII. For the numismatic evidence, I have used the list of magistrates in Thompson, NSSCA pp. 546-599, supplemented by D.M. Lewis, "The Chronology of the Athenian New Style Coinage," NC 7th series 2 (1962) pp. 275-300 (hereafter referred to as Lewis) and H.B. Mattingly, "Some Third Magistrates in the Athenian New Style Silver Coinage," JHS 91 (1971) pp. 85-93. The preponderance of evidence persuades me that the lower dating of the coinage advocated by Lewis, Mattingly, and most recently, by Badian (AJAH 1, 1976, pp. 117-119) is substantially correct and I have adopted it below. Although no index has yet been published for ID, I have attempted to trace down each name as thoroughly as possible in the Delian evidence. Doubtless names have been missed, but, I hope, not too many. Through the kindness of Professor and Mrs. B.D. Meritt and Professor Homer Thompson, I have also (in 1970) searched each name through the card index of known Athenians which is housed at the Institute for Advanced Study in Princeton.

Of particular use in compiling this index have been the following additional books and articles:

K. Clinton, "The Sacred Officials of the Eleusinian Mysteries," _Trans. Am. Philosoph. Soc._ 64 (1974).

W.S. Ferguson, "The Oligarchic Revolution at Athens of the Year 103/2 B.C.," _Klio_ 4 (1904) pp. 1-17.

__________, "Researches in Athenian and Delian Documents I, III," _Klio_ 7 (1907) pp. 213-240; 9 (1909) pp. 304-340.

__________, _Hellenistic Athens_ (London, 1911).

J. Kirchner, _Inscriptiones Graecae_, II-III, editio minor (Berlin, 1913-1940).

P. Roussel, _Délos colonie athénienne_ (Paris, 1916).

__________, _Les cultes égyptiens à Délos du IIIe au Ier siècle av. J.-C._ (Paris, 1916).

A[ca.4]ης Θορίκ[ιος]

Priest of Sarapis in 102/1 (II^2 2336_{83}).

'Αγαθοκλῆς 'Αγκυλῆ[θ]εν

PA 53. Priest of Artemis on the Island in 103/2 (II^2 2336_{39}). His son, Lysimachos, was chosen to be a pompostolos in ca. 100 (ID 2608_{12}).

'Αγαθοκλῆς Σω[σ]ικρά[το]υ Οἰναῖος

PA 69. στρατηγὸς ἐπὶ τὴν παρασκευὴν τὴν ἐν ἄστει in 97/6 (II^2 2336_{263}).

'Αθηνόδωρος 'Αθηνογένου Α[ἰξ]ωνεύς

Herald of the Council of the Areopagos in 99/8 (II^2 2336_{181}). His son, Athenodoros (PA 266), is attested as Thesmothetes in 88/7 (II^2 1714_{9}).

'Αλέξανδρος

PA 489. ἀγορανόμος in 101/0 (II^2 2336_{113}).

['Α]λκιβιάδης Ποτάμιος

PA 596. Thesmothetes in 102/1 (II^2 2336_{59}).

'Αμμώνιος [Δημητρίο]υ 'Αναφλύστιος

NPA p. 11. Epimeletes of Delos in 107/6 (ID 2232_{4-5}; his name, however, has been erased); Hoplite General in 103/2 (II^2

2336_{6}). From a distinguished family (see the stemma in Roussel, DCA p. 104), his uncle, Dionysios, was Archon in 128/7; his brothers, Dionysios and Demetrios, held respectively the following offices: Priest of Apollo sometime before 111/0 (ID 1959), Epimeletes of Delos in 111/0 (ID 2125), Hoplite General in 106/5 (FD III 2 no. 5_{12}); Priest of Sarapis in 111/0 (ID 2070, 2125, and 2610_{34}), Priest of Apollo in 98/7 (II^{2} 2336_{148}). It is noteworthy that Ammonios seems to have followed his brother, Dionysios, by a few years in holding the important offices of Epimeletes of Delos and of Hoplite General. His sons Demetrios and Dionysios participated in the Pythaïs of 98/7 as ephebes (FD III 2 no. 26_{4-5} = Hesperia Suppl. 15 p. 57). See Hesperia 47 (1978) p. 284, Agora XV 240_{51}, and Trans. Am. Philosoph. Soc. 64 (1974) p. 51_{26-27} for other members of this family.

'Αμμώνιος ('Αμμωνίου) <Π>αμβωτάδης

PA 725. Priest of Apollo on Delos in 103/2 (II^{2} 2336_{37}, ID 1656). In the following year he took part in the celebration of the Pythian games and was honored by the Delphians for his distinguished service to Apollo (FD III 1 no. 228). His grandfather 'A.'A.Π. (PA 724), one of the original cleruchs to Delos, is known as guarantor of a loan (ID 1416 II B_{88-89}) in 156 and as Gymnasiarch on Delos for the year 156/5 (ID 2589_{17}). For a stemma, see HThR 30 (1937) p. 222.

['Αμφικρ]άτης 'Επιστράτου Περιθοίδης

PA 774. Much of the financial organization of the Pythaïds of 106/5 and 98/7 seems to have been entrusted to this man. In charge of the ἀπαρχαί for the Pythaïs of 106/5 (FD III 2 no. $13_{20\ II}$), he was elected, it appears in 106/5, to oversee the arrangements for the next Pythaïs and in general to set in motion the machinery for sending the Pythaïds to Delphi every eight years (FD III 2 no. 54 [as re-edited by Daux, Delphes p. 557 and restudied by Tracy, BCH 99, 1975, pp. 195-196] and II^2 2336_{2-3}). This charge was a complex one which entailed overseeing both the dispatch of the Pythaïs and the collection of funds (supra, p. 149). In the actual celebration of 98/7, Amphikrates exercised a role of ceremonial importance as the escort of the Holy Tripod and Firebearer to and from Delphi (FD III 2 no. 32). Significantly he also served in ca. 101 as first mint magistrate with his brother Epistratos as second magistrate (Lewis, p. 291). His brother is attested as Secretary to the corps of ephebes in 102/1 (II^2 $1028_{54,\ 253-255}$ = Hesperia Suppl. 15 pp. 33-40).

'Ανδρέας 'Ανδρέου [Πειραιεύς]

PA 838. Known on Delos in 119/8 as an adjunct member of the ephebic corps (ID 2598_{54}); Herald of the Council of the Areopagos in 97/6 (II^2 2336_{246}); Epimeletes of Delos ca. 90 (ID 2266_{7}).

'Αντικράτης [Φιλίσκο]υ 'Επικηφίσιος

PA 1082. Listed among a number of Athenians prominent on Delos in ca. 110 (ID 2630_{20}); Priest of Apollo on Delos in 101/0 (II^2 2336_{122}); Polemarch in 97/6 (II^2 2336_{249}). Thompson (NSSCA p. 551) thinks it highly likely that he is identical with the mint magistrate PA 1077.

'Αντίπατρος Κυδα[θηναιεύς]

PA 1170. Polemarch in 101/0 (II^2 2336_{96}). The grave marker of his son Ζήνων is extant (II^2 6576). Cf. also II^2 2458_7.

'Απο[λλό]δωρος Δ̣[_ca.7_]

PA 1430. Hoplite General in 101/0 (II^2 2336_{93}). Since it is an observable fact in this period that those who attained the Hoplite Generalship also held the post of Epimeletes of Delos, it appears quite probable that this man is identical with 'Α. Φιλωνύμου Δεκελεεύς (PA 1414) who was Epimeletes of the Island about 110 (ID 2615_5).

'Απολλωνίδης Λακιάδ[η]ς

PA 1494. Thesmothetes in 101/0 (II^2 2336_{101}).

'Απολλώνιος

PA 1508. Thesmothetes in 103/2 (II^2 2336_{18}).

'Απο[λλ]ώνιος Νικάνδρου Κυθήρριος

PA 1542. Thesmothetes in 98/7 (II^2 2336$_{195}$, FD III 2 nos. 10 and 2$_{19}$ = Hesperia Suppl. 15 p. 50). He is probably identical with the proxenos and euergetes of the inhabitants of Thera attested in IG XII 3 Suppl. 1297, 1298.

'Αργεῖος 'Α[σκλαπιώνος 'Ατ]ηνεύς

PA 1584. Speaker of a decree ca. 120 (Kerameikos III A 6$_2$); Thesmothetes in 97/6 (II^2 2336$_{256}$). The Taxiarch of 161/0 (II^2 956$_{50}$) and the Herald of the Council and Demos of 135/4 (Agora XV 243$_{51-52}$) are without doubt relatives, but not identical with this man (as Meritt-Traill in the index to Agora XV).

'Αργεῖος 'Αργείου Τρικορύσιος

PA 1586. ἐπὶ τὰ ἱερά in 109/8 (SEG XVI nos. 452-453). Archon in 98/7 (II^2 2336$_{192}$, FD III 2 nos. 10 and 2$_{15}$ = Hesperia Suppl. 15 p. 50) and ex officio Archetheoros of the Archons in the Pythaïs of 98/7 (FD III 2 nos. 10 and 2$_{31}$); General ἐπὶ τὸν Πειραιᾶ ca. 100 (II^2 2872, 2952). His son, Argeios, appears to have taken part in the Pythaïs of 98/7 as a child pythaïst (FD III 2 nos. 31 and 17$_{64}$ = Hesperia Suppl. 15 p. 54). A descendant of the Archon is attested some 80 years later as active in the Genos of the Kerykes (Trans. Am. Philosoph. Soc. 64, 1974, p. 51$_{19}$) and a forbearer is attested as a councillor of Aiantis in 223/2 (Agora XV 127$_{25}$).

'Αριστίων Εὐδόξου Μελιτεύς

PA 1747. Ephebe in 128/7 (*Hesperia* 24, 1955, p. 232_{217}, *FD* III 2 no. $24_{22\ III}$); Priest of Sarapis on Delos in 114/3 (*ID* 2208, 2610_{30}); Polemarch in 98/7 (II^2 2336_{194}, *FD* III 2 nos. 10 and 2_{17} = *Hesperia* Suppl. 15 p. 50).

'Αριστιών Σωκράτου ἐξ Οἴου

PA 1749. ἐπιμελητῆς ἐμπορίου in 101/0 (II^2 2336_{111}); Epimeletes of Delos in 97/6 (II^2 2336_{229}, *ID* 1878_{2-3}, 1892). His father, Sokrates (*PA* 13119), was Epimeletes of Delos in 117/6 (*ID* 2055_{19-20}), is attested in a catalog of prominent men on Delos (*ID* 2630_{3}), and proposed three decrees in Athens during 118/7 (II^2 $1008_{4,\ 52}$, *Agora* XV 253_{6}).

'Αριστόνους Πρωτάρχου Σφήττιος

PA 2041. Priest of ἁγνῆς θεοῦ on Delos in 101/0 (II^2 2336_{132}). Lewis (p. 287) identifies him with the third mint magistrate of 88/7. If this is correct, he was a strong supporter of Mithridates. His son, Philoxenos, was an ephebe in 102/1 (II^2 1028_{181} = *Hesperia* Suppl. 15 p. 38).

'Αρίστων Π[ανταχ]λέους Γαργήττιος

PA 2155. Basileus in 97/6 (II^2 2336_{248}). See II^2 5947 for an ancestor.

'Αριστώνυμος (Φανίου) 'Ελευσίνιος

PA 2193. Speaker of a decree in 106/5 (II^2 1011_{53}); Thesmothetes in 102/1 (II^2 2336_{56}); General ἐπὶ τὸν Πειραιᾶ ca. 100 (Hesperia 36, 1967, pp. $88\text{-}91_{38\text{-}40}$). His father, Φανίας, was a councillor in 135/4 (Agora XV 243_{64}) and his brother 'Αρχῖνος is known from a statue base on the Acropolis (II^2 4102 A).

'Αρτεμίδωρος Βερενικίδης

PA 2266. Thesmothetes in 101/0 (II^2 2336_{99}).

'Αρχίας Διογένου 'Αναφλύστιος

PA 2461 and PA 2453. ἐπιμελητὴς ἐμπορίου in 99/8 (II^2 2336_{177}); General ἐπὶ τὸ ναυτικόν in 101/0(?) (II^2 2336_{259}).

'Αρχ[ίας] 'Αρχεστράτου Κυδαθηναιεύς

PA 1600. στρατηγὸς ἐπὶ τὸ ναυτικόν in 97/6(?) (II^2 2336_{267}).

'Αρχωνίδης Ναυκράτου ἐκ Κεραμέω[ν]

PA 2575; stemma under PA 10531. Pythaïst ἐκ Κηρύκων in 106/5 (FD III 2 no. 13_{11}); Basileus in 98/7 (II^2 2336_{193}, FD III 2 nos. 10 and 2_{16} = Hesperia Suppl. 15 p. 50 where, however, his patronymic is given mistakenly as Ναυσιστράτου). His brother, Nausistratos, was ὁ ἐπὶ τὰ ἱερά on Delos in 110/9 (ID 2220_6) and his son, also named Nausistratos, was an ephebe in ca. 80 (II^2 $1039_{81\ II}$).

'Ασκληπιά[δης] ('Ικεσίου) ['Αλαι]εύς

PA 2587; stemma infra, p. 197. Priest of Dionysos in 101/0 (II^2 2336_{126}). He should be identified with 'Α. 'Ικεσίου 'Αθηναῖος who was victorious as a dramatic poet at Tanagra in ca. 90 (IG VII 540_{12} + SEG 19 $335_{12, 18, 41}$). He also served as a mint magistrate with his father in ca. 103 (Lewis, p. 293). The Asklepiades son of Hikesios who served as hieromnemon at Delphi in ca. 125 (FD III 2 69_3 = II^2 1134_5)[1] and was also both a tragic poet and Priest of Dionysos (FD III 2 $69_{23, 39}$) must, seemingly, be his uncle rather than be identical with him (as Lewis, p. 293 and G.M. Sifakis, Studies in the History of Hellenistic Drama [London, 1967] p. 25). Demeas of Halai, Epimeletes of Piraeus (II^2 2336_{23}) and Epimeletes of Delos (ID 2255), was probably his brother and Demetrios son of Asklepides of Halai, Priest of Roma (II^2 2336_{265}), his first cousin. Lineal descendants are Megiste daughter of Asklepides of Halai, Priestess of Athena Polias in ca. 25 B.C. (II^2 3173_4), and Seleukos son of Demeas of Halai, active in the Genos of the Kerykes ca. 20 B.C. (Trans. Am. Philosoph. Soc. 64, 1974, p. 51_{30}).

Βάκχιος 'Αχαρνεύς

PA 2829. Thesmothetes in 102/1 (II^2 2336_{58}).

---

[1]II^2 1134 was inscribed by a mason whose known work dates 131/0-117/6 (GRBS 11, 1970, pp. 330-331); thus a date ca. 125 seems inevitable.

Βούλων Λ[εωστ]ράτου Παλληνεύς

PA 2920; NPA p. 43. Participated in the Pythaïds of 128/7, 106/5, and 98/7 respectively as a child pythaïst (FD III 2 no. $12_{5\ IV}$), as a knight (Ibid. no. $28_{22\ III}$), and as Thesmothetes (Ibid. nos. 10 and 2_{23} = Hesperia Suppl. 15 p. 50); he is also known as Thesmothetes from II^2 2336_{199}.

Βύτταкος (Πύρρου) Λαμπτρεύς

PA 2934; stemma in Roussel, DCA p. 102. Third mint magistrate in ca. 118/7 (Thompson, NSSCA p. 557 with Mattingly, JHS 91, 1971, p. 91); knight in the Pythaïs of 106/5 (FD III 2 no. 28_{16});[2] Gymnasiarch on Delos in 104/3 (ID 2599); Epimeletes of the Piraeus in 102/1 (II^2 2336_{87}). He or his nephew is mentioned in an Athenian catalog in ca. 95/4 (II^2 2460_{10}). His grandfather is known as Epimeletes of Delos in 153/2 (ID 1432 $Aa_{3\ I}$) and as Agonothetes Theseorum ca. 140 (II^2 963_9), his uncle as ὁ ἐπὶ τὰ ἱερά in ca. 135 (ID 2041), and his brother Πύρρος as Epimeletes of the Island in 104/3 (ID 2599; cf. sub nomine).

---

[2]Note that the Buttakos who was a knight in the Pythaïs of 128/7 (FD III 2 no. 27_{17}) was not the present man (as Roussel, DCA p. 102 and Sundwall, NPA p. 43), but rather his uncle, Buttakos (III) son of Buttakos of Lamptrai (see FD III 2 no. 37 and the addition on p. 290).

Γάι[ος Γαΐου 'Αχαρνεύ]ς

Priest of Holy Aphrodite on Delos in 97/6 (II^2 2336_{238}; ID 2240, which also records a daughter Νικόπολις). He is either identical with, or the son of PA 2937, who was Priest of the Great Gods in 128/7 (ID 1900) and Priest of Sarapis in 115/4 (ID 2079). A second daughter is attested (II^2 1942_{10} = Hesperia Suppl. 15 p. 79).

Γλαυκία[ς] ('Ηρακλείδου) [Κρι]ωεύς

PA 2966. Herald εἰς Δῆλον in 103/2 (II^2 2336_{44}). His family is prominent among the Dionysiac artists. He participated in the Pythaïs of 98/7 as theoros, paean singer, and κωμῳδός (FD III 2 no. $48_{16, 21, 46}$ = Hesperia Suppl. 15 pp. 60-63). His father, Herakleides, was Archetheoros of the Technitai in the Pythaïs of 128/7 (FD III 2 no. 47_7) and a few years earlier contributed in his own name and in his son's for repairs to the theater in Piraeus (II^2 2334_{14}).

Δάμων (Φιλοκλέους) ['Ικ]αριεύς

PA 3139. Gymnasiarch on Delos in 97/6 (II^2 2336_{269}); ὁ ἐπὶ τὰ ἱερά ca. 92 (ID 2507_{13}).

Δεινίας Παλληνεύς

PA 3168. ἐπὶ τὰ ἱερά in 101/0 (II^2 2336_{115}).

Δημέας 'Α[λαιεύς]

PA 3311. Epimeletes of the Harbor in Piraeus in 103/2 (II^2 2336$_{23}$); identical with Δ. 'Ικεσίου 'Α. , who was Epimeletes of Delos in ca. 90 (ID 2045, 2255). See stemma on next page for other members of his family.

Δημήτ[ριος _ _ _] (Αἰγεῖδος)

PA 3347. Priest of Zeus Kynthios in 102/1 (II^2 2336$_{85}$).

Δημ<ή>τρι<ο>ς (Δημητρίου) Αἰ<ξ>ω[νεύ]ς

PA 3371. Priest of Roma in 101/0 (II^2 2336$_{128}$); Gymnasiarch on Delos in 98/7 (ID 1929$_{5-6}$). His father contributed for the repair of the theater in Piraeus ca. 150 (II^2 2334$_{16}$). His brother, Dionysios, held the post of General ἐπὶ τὴν παρασκευήν in 99/8 (II^2 2336$_{179}$). His son Λεόντιος is attested as a pompostolos in ca. 100 (ID 2607$_{10}$). Kephisodoros of Aixone q.v. may be another kinsman.

Δημήτριος 'Ασκληπίδου 'Αλαιεύς

PA 3374. Priest of Roma in 97/6 (II^2 2336$_{265}$). See the stemma under Demeas of Halai.

Δημήτριος Δημ[ητρί]ο̣υ 'Αναφλύσ[τιος]

PA 3385; see Roussel, DCA p. 104 for stemma. Priest of Sarapis in 111/0 (ID 2610$_{34}$ and 2125); Priest of Apollo on Delos in 100/99 (II^2 2336$_{148}$). The family is a distinguished one; his brothers, Ammonios and Dionysios, both held the offices of

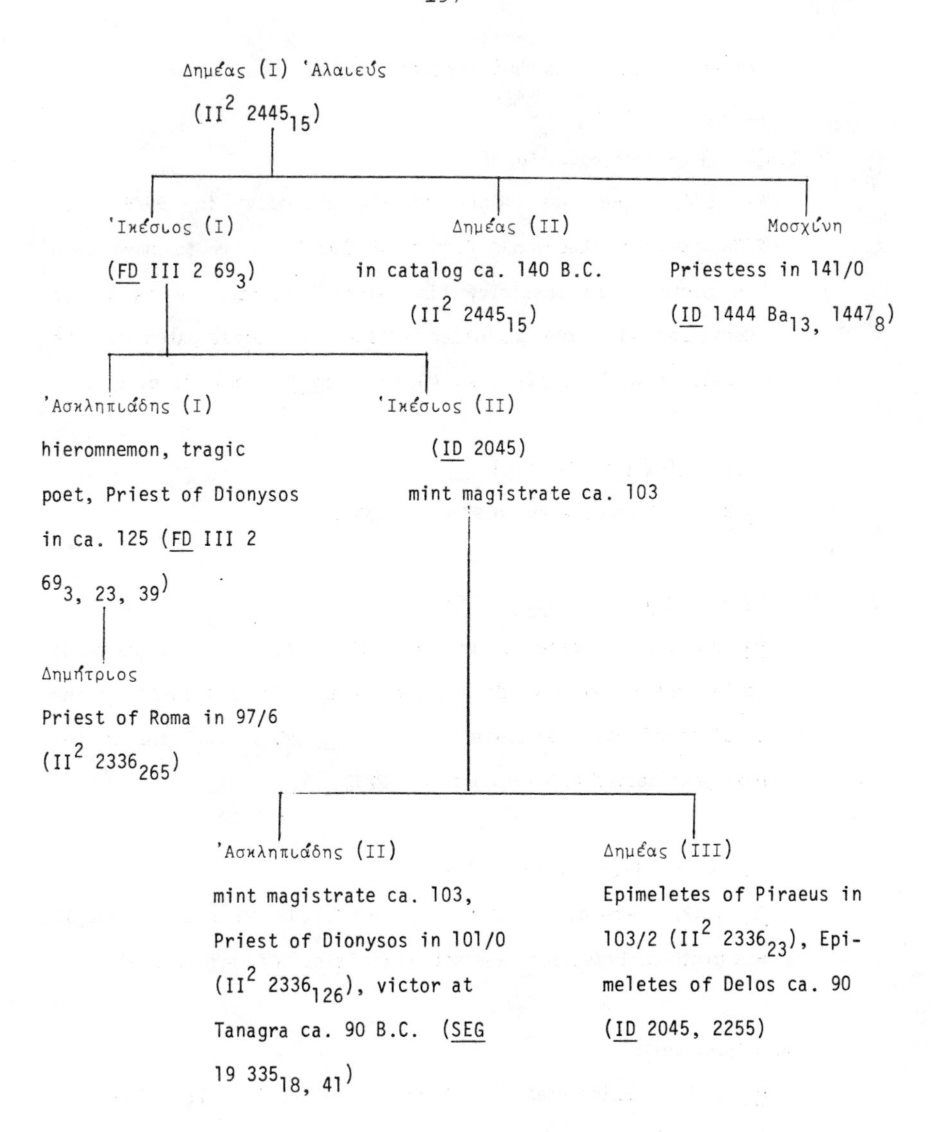
Δημέας (I) Ἁλαιεύς
(II2 2445 15)
Ἱκέσιος (I)
(FD III 2 69 3)
Δημέας (II)
in catalog ca. 140 B.C.
(II2 2445 15)
Μοσχύνη
Priestess in 141/0
(ID 1444 Ba 13, 1447 8)
Ἀσκληπιάδης (I)
hieromnemon, tragic
poet, Priest of Dionysos
in ca. 125 (FD III 2
69 3, 23, 39)
Ἱκέσιος (II)
(ID 2045)
mint magistrate ca. 103
Δημήτριος
Priest of Roma in 97/6
(II2 2336 265)
Ἀσκληπιάδης (II)
mint magistrate ca. 103,
Priest of Dionysos in 101/0
(II2 2336 126), victor at
Tanagra ca. 90 B.C. (SEG
19 335 18, 41)
Δημέας (III)
Epimeletes of Piraeus in
103/2 (II2 2336 23), Epi-
meletes of Delos ca. 90
(ID 2045, 2255)

Epimeletes of Delos and Hoplite General (see under Ἀμμώνιος Δ. Ἀ.).

[Δη]μ̣[ήτ]ριος Θεοδοσίου Λακιάδης

PA 6763. He was Agoranomos(?), probably in 99/8 (II^2 2336$_{226}$). The Eponymous Archon of 100/99 seems to have been his brother or, possibly, his father. Perhaps he is to be identified with the Dionysiac artist who participated in the Pythaïs of 98/7 (FD III 2 no. 48$_{49}$ = Hesperia Suppl. 15 p. 62).

Δημήτριος Δ[ca.6 Παι]ονί[δη]ς

PA 3434. Thesmothetes in 97/6 (II^{2}2336$_{253}$).

Διογένης [ca.4 Κυδαθ]ηναιεύ̣ς

PA 3834. Thesmothetes in 97/6 (II^{2}2336$_{252}$). His daughter Zoila contributed towards the construction of a theater in the precinct of Holy Aphrodite in 108/7 (ID 2628$_{39\ III}$) and in the next year served as kanephoros (ID 2232$_{7-8}$).

Διονύσιος Δημη[τρίου Αἰξ]ων[εύς]

PA 4142. General ἐπὶ τὴν παρασκευήν in 99/8 (II^{2}2336$_{179}$). His brother, Demetrios, was active on Delos (cf. sub nomine).

Διονύσιος Παλληνεύς

PA 4232. Epimeletes of Piraeus in 100/99 (II^2 2336$_{145}$). Several Dionysioi of Pallene are attested; it is impossible to know with which, if any, he is to be identified.

Διονύσιος Χ̣[_ _ _ _ _]

<u>PA</u> 4116. Thesmothetes in 103/2 (II^2 2336_{17}). Dow restored Χ[ολαργεύς] rather than Χ[ολλείδης], presumably on the assumption that the Thesmothetai were listed in tribal order. If this assumption is correct and, in this instance, it appears doubtful, for the Thesmothetai were not listed in tribal order in the second year, then Cholleidai which belongs to Leontis, the 4th tribe in this period, is indeed impossible and Cholargos which belongs to Akamantis, the 6th tribe, becomes the only possibility. The <u>nomen</u> Dionysios is well attested in both demes: for Cholargos, see <u>Hesperia</u> 34 (1965) p. 91_{21}; <u>Agora</u> XV 373_{62-63}; <u>NPA</u> p. 62; for Cholleidai, see <u>PA</u> 4267, <u>Agora</u> XV 129_{77}.

The reading of X, however, is very doubtful. See epigraphical commentary <u>ad</u> <u>loc</u>.

Διονυσογένης 'Ανα[γ]υ̣ράσιος

<u>PA</u> 4273. General ἐπὶ τὴν παρασκευήν in 101/0 (II^2 2336_{105}). His son, Θυμοτέλης, is attested as a pompostolos on Delos in ca. 100 B.C. (<u>ID</u> 2607_9). The Διονυσι (<u>sic</u>)γένης 'Α. who appears in a list of contributors of 183/2 (II^2 2332_{64}) is undoubtedly a relative, probably his grandfather.

Διονυσόδωρος (Διονυσοδώρου) Δειρ̣[αδιώτη]ς

<u>PA</u> 4292; see stemma under <u>PA</u> 12836. Gymnasiarch εἰς Δῆλον in 101/0 (II^2 2336_{118}). His son is attested in a catalog of Leontis (II^2 2461_{39}) and his brother, Σοφοκλῆς (<u>PA</u> 12836),

was Priest of Asklepios (II^2 4457). His brother's son, Philotas, served as Polemarch in 88/7 (II^2 1714_4). Lineal descendants are attested in ca. 20 in the Genos of the Kerykes (Trans. Am. Philosoph. Soc. 64, 1974, p. $51_{23, 27}$).

[Διοσκουρίδης]

PA 4344. Epimeletes of Delos in 103/2 (II^2 2336_{25}, ID 1927).

Διότιμος Μαραθώνιος

PA 4390. Polemarch in 102/1 (II^2 2336_{54}). His brother, Ζηνίων, participated as a knight in the Pythaïs of 106/5 (FD III 2 no. $28_{15\ III}$) and his brother's son, Diotimos, was an ephebe in 102/1 (II^2 1028_{214} = Hesperia Suppl. 15 p. 38). For another possible descendant, see II^2 1339_5.

Διόφ[αν]τος ('Αριστοκλέους) Μαραθώ(νιος)

PA 4433. Priest of the Holy Goddess in 103/2 (II^2 2336_{43}, ID 2235, 2236, and 2245); ἐπὶ τὰ ἱερά in 99/8 (II^2 2336_{217}, ID 1709); Priest of Zeus Kynthios in 94/3 (ID 1887, 1889). The Diophantos son of Diophantos of Marathon attested a Priest of the Great Gods on Delos (ID 1904) is probably his son.

[Δ]ράκων (Φλυεύς)

Priest of Sarapis on Delos in 103/2 (II^2 2336_{42}, ID 2129 and 2156). His daughter, Κοσμώ, is known as a kanephoros in 103/2 (ID 2156). His grandfather, Δ. Δράκοντος Φ., appears to have been one of the original cleruchs; he acted as guarantor of a loan in 155 (ID 1417 C_{96}) and as a priest in 154/3 (ID 1499_{17}).

Δωσίθεος

PA 4625. Thesmothetes in 103/2 (II^2 2336_{16}).

Δωσίθεος (Προτίμου) [ἐ]γ Μυρρινού[τ]της

PA 4630; stemma under II^2 3488. Thesmothetes in 100/99 (II^2 2336_{156}). His uncle, Dositheos, served as hierope of the Apollonia on Delos in 143/2 (ID 2593_8); his son, Protimos, was Epimeletes of Delos ca. 85 (ID 1604). The Dositheos of Myrrhinouta attested as a tamias in the early part of the second century B.C. (Ath. Mitt. 67, 1942, 25_8) was probably his grandfather.

Ἑρμοκλῆς [ca.5]ο[_ _ _]

PA 5145. Agoranomos on Delos in 103/2 (II^2 2336_{32}).

Ἑστιαῖος [Θε]οχάριδος ἐκ Κεραμέων

PA 5202. Hoplite General in 100/99 (II^2 2336_{139}); he seems to have been Agoranomos on Delos in 101/0 (II^2 2336_{113}). He was formerly (in PA 5202 and NPA p. 73) thought to have served as ἐπὶ τὰ ἱερά in 112/1, but ID 2229 and 2248 reveal that this was a different man. His cousin, Theokharis (PA 7188), was also active in this period both in Athens and on Delos; cf. sub nomine.

Εὐκ[τ]ί̣μ̣ε[νος Εὐδή]μου Εἰτεαῖος

PA 5772. [N.B. Number 5772 in PA should be deleted and this entry should be added as PA 5805a]. Priest of Sarapis in 97/6 (II^2 2336_{261}). His homonymous grandfather is known as orator, treasurer, and secretary of prytaneis in 140/39 (Agora XV $240_{26-27,\ 41,\ 46}$). His brother is probably the Eudemos who is attested as a knight in the Pythaïs of 106/5 (FD III 2 no. $28_{21\ III}$); his nephew was an ephebe in 102/1 (II^2 1028_{238} = Hesperia Suppl. 15 p. 39).

Ἐχεκράτης [Τρινεμ]ε̣εύς

PA 6173. Archon in 102/1 (II^2 $2336_{49,\ 52}$, II^2 1028_{131} = Hesperia Suppl. 15 p. 38).

Ζή[ν]ων (Διονυσίου) [Κ]ηφισιεύς

Priest of Zeus Kynthios in 103/2 (II^2 2336_{45}, ID 1885). One son, Dionysios (PA 4190), was ὑφιερεύς of Sarapis in 109/8 (SEG XVI no. 452 and ID 2065) and another, Zeno (PA 6212), served as kleidoukhos of Holy Aphrodite in 107/6 (ID 2232_6). His brother Apollophanes was Priest of Sarapis in 109/8 (SEG XVI no. 452). The stemma, as given by Roussel at ID 1885, should be augmented as follows:

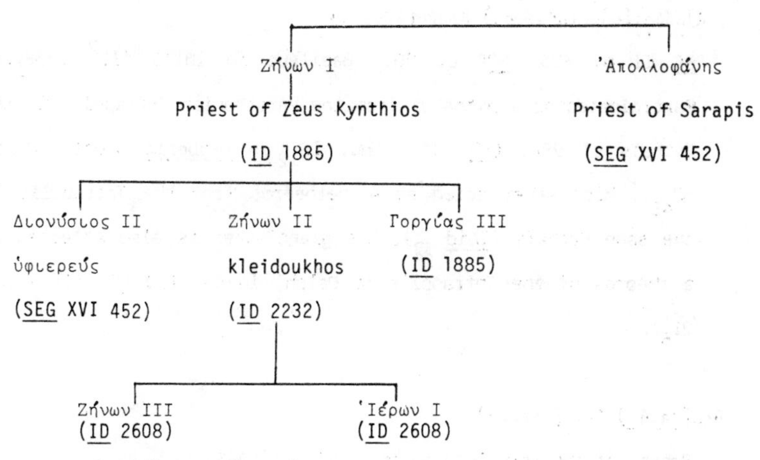

Ζήνων 'Αρί̣σ[τωνος Μ]αραθώνιος

PA 6218. Thesmothetes in 97/6 (II^2 2336$_{255}$). The family is well known; see the stemmata in PA 2165 and NPA p. 85. His father served as an emissary of the Athenian Dionysiac artists to the Amphictyonic Council in 130/29 (II^2 1132$_{48, 73}$); his brother, Ariston, was Gymnasiarch on Delos in 118/7 (ID 2589$_{59}$), and his nephew, Zeno, is attested as an ephebe in 102/1 (II^2 1028$_{223}$ = Hesperia Suppl. 15 p. 38). The family was very prominent in the post-Sullan period, with at least one member (PA 6220) becoming Epimeletes of Delos (ID 1663) and another (PA 11520) Hoplite General (II^2 3173).

'Η̣[ρ]άκλειτος 'Ηρ̣[_ca.7_] Σφήττιος

PA 6503. Archon in 97/6 (II^2 2336$_{247}$, II^2 1029$_4$).

[ʽΗ]ρόδοτ[ο]ς (Ζήνωνος) Προβα[λίσιος]

PA II p. 605; NPA p. 90. Basileus in 101/0 (II^2 2336$_{95}$). Participated as a pythaïst from the Marathonian Tetrapolis in the Pythaïs of 98/7 (FD III 2 no. 10$_{12}$ = Hesperia Suppl. 15 p. 50$_{45}$); his father acted as Archetheoros from the Tetrapolis in the same Pythaïs (Ibid.$_{39}$); his grandfather is also attested as a theoros of the Tetrapolis to Delphi in ca. 150 (FD III 2 no. 21$_{6}$).

Θεα[ca.6] 'Αγγ[ελῆθεν]

Priest of the Holy Goddess in 102/1 (II^2 2336$_{84}$).

Θεόβιος Διονυσίου 'Αχαρνεύς

PA 6674. Priest of Sarapis in 101/0 (II^2 2336$_{134}$, ID 2067); Priest of Holy Aphrodite in 99/8 or 98/7 (II^2 2336$_{219}$, ID 2265); Priest of Zeus Kynthios in 97/6 (II^2 2336$_{242}$, ID 1878).

Θεοδόσιος Λακιάδης

PA 6762. Archon in 100/99 (II^2 2336$_{137, 152}$). Θ. Δίου Λ., Priest of Apollo Patroös and of the mystic house of his genos (II^2 2871), is either identical with the Archon or, more probably, his father. Δημήτριος Θ. Λ, q.v., seems to be either his brother or his son.

Θεόδοτ[ος _ _ _]

Priest of Dionysos in 102/1 (II^2 2336$_{79}$).

[Θεόδο]τος (Διοδώρου) Σουνιεύς

PA 6803. Priest of the Syrian Divinities on Delos ca. 113/2 (ID 2261, 2285); Priest of Holy Aphrodite in 110/09 (ID 2228 with ID 2626); orator of a decree honoring ephebes in 106/5 (II^2 $1011_{5, 33}$) among whom appears his son Timokrates (II^2 $1011_{99\ V}$); in the same year, he also very probably (the text is emended) spoke in favor of honoring Hyrcanus I (Jos. A.I. 14.152; see A Wilhelm, Philologus 60, 1901, p. 487ff. and Day, An Economic History pp. 86-87); two years later he proposed a decree in honor of prytaneis (Agora XV 254_7); in 102/1 he was Epimeletes of Delos (II^2 2336_{64}, ID 1562). His father is attested in an association of Syrians ca. 150 (II^2 2358_{22}).

Θεοκλῆς

PA 6933. Archon in 103/2 (II^2 $2336_{5, 10}$, II^2 1335).

Θεόμνηστος (Θεογένου) [Κυδα]θηναιεύ[ς]

PA 6968. Priest of Sarapis in 105/4 (ID 2080, 2128, 2155); Priest of Artemis on the Island in 102/1 (II^2 2336_{82}).

[Θ]εόπομπος Κεφ[αλῆθ]ε[ν]

PA 7033. Thesmothetes in 102/1 (II^2 2336_{61}).

Θεότιμος Αἰξωνεύς

PA 7061. ἐπὶ τὴν φυλακὴν τῶν ἱερῶν χρημάτων in 103/2 (II^2 2336_{34}). For his grandfather, Theotimos, who appears in a list of contributors of 164/3, see Hesperia 36, 1967, p. 89_{15}.

Θεόχαρις ['Εστιαίου] ἐκ Κεραμέων

PA 7188. Kosmetes of ephebes in 119/8 (II^2 1008$_{46}$); Herald of the Council of the Areopagos in 101/0 (II^2 2336$_{103}$); ἐπὶ τὰ ἱερά in 99/8 (II^2 2336$_{203}$, ID 1709$_{10}$). 'Ε. Θ. ἐκ Κ., Hoplite General in 100/99 (II^2 2336$_{139}$), appears to be his cousin.

Θέων 'Ερχιεύς

PA 7217. Thesmothetes in 102/1 (II^2 2336$_{57}$).

Θέων Παιονίδης

PA 7220. ἐπὶ τὰ ἱερὰ in 109/8 (SEG XVI nos. 452-453); Nauarch in 100/99 (II^2 2336$_{146}$).

'Ιασ[ων _ _ _ _]

PA 7428. στρατηγὸς ἐπὶ τὴν παρασκευὴν in 103/2 (II^2 2336$_{21}$).

Καλλί[ας] 'Αθμον[εύς]

Director of the Public Bank on Delos in 102/1 (II^2 2336$_{78}$). II^2 5341 and II^2 5339 of the first century A.D. probably record descendants.

Καλλίμαχος ('Επικράτου) Λευκονοεύς

PA 8021; stemma in NPA p. 105 (see also Roussel, DCA p. 115). Basileus in 100/99 (II^2 2336$_{153}$) and mint magistrate in 93/2 (Lewis, p. 277). His son Epikrates (PA 4903) is attested as a child pythaïst in 106/5 (FD III 2 no. 15$_{14\ III}$), mint magistrate sometime after Sulla on the lower dating (cf. Thompson, NSSCA p. 564), and. Herald of the Areopagos in ca. 55 (II^2 1720_9 with Hesperia 3, 1934, pp. 150-153); his grandson, Kallimachos, was Epimeletes of Delos in ca. 60 B.C. according to Roussel, DCA p. 115 (ID 2205, 2161) and his great-grandson, Epikrates, was Archon (II^2 4714), priest in the Genos of the Kerykes in 20/19 (Trans. Am. Philosoph. Soc. 64, 1974, p. 51_9), Herald of the Council of the Areopagos in 14/3 (II^2 1721_{15}), and Hoplite General twice (IG XII.8.26_{5-6}).

Καλλίστρατ[ος ca.4]εύς

PA 8141. Epimeletes of Delos in 101/0 (II^2 2336_{109}).

Κηφισ[_ _ _ _]

Nauarch in 103/2 (II^2 2336_{19}).

Κηφισόδωρος Αἰ[ξων]εύς

PA 8359. Epimeletes of Piraeus in 101/0 (II^2 2336_{107}). It would appear that he is identical with Κ. Δημητρίου Α. who is attested as στρατηγήσας ἐπ' Ἴμβρον in ca. 100 (Hesperia 36, 1967, p. 89_{41-44}) and with the Κ.Δ. of the tribe Kekropis who was an ephebe in 128/7 (FD III 2 no. $24_{20\ I}$ with Hesperia 24, 1955, p. 232_{211}).

[Κιχη]σίας Σουνιεύς

NPA pp. 110-111. Agoranomos on Delos in 103/2 (II^2 2336$_{31}$). His sons, Κιχησίας and Πραξικλῆς, acted as pompostoloi on Delos in ca. 100 (ID 2608$_{8-9}$).

Κλειτόμαχος [_ca.7_] Φλυεύς

PA 8542. Thesmothetes in 97/6 (II^2 2336$_{254}$). He is perhaps identical with the knight of Ptolemaiïs who is attested as a participant in the Pythaïs of 106/5 (FD III 2 no. 28$_{45\ I}$).

Λακρατείδη[ς Σωστ]ράτου Ἰκαριεύς

PA 8971; stemma under PA 13354 with NPA p. 59. He is first attested in a list of prominent men dated ca. 120 (II^2 2452$_{41}$); next at Eleusis ca. 110 as ἱερεὺς θεοῦ καὶ θεᾶς καὶ Εὐβουλεῶς making a dedication to Demeter and Kore on behalf of himself, his sons Sostratos and Dionysios, and his wife Dionysia (II^2 4701); lastly as Thesmothetes in 98/7 (II^2 2336$_{200}$, FD III 2 nos. 10 and 2$_{24}$ = Hesperia Suppl. 15 p. 50). His son Dionysios was an ephebe in 106/5 (FD III 2 no. 25$_{9\ I}$). The Σώστρατος Λακρατείδου Ἰκαριεύς, who participated in the same Pythaïs as a pythaïst chosen by lot (II^2 1941$_7$, FD III 2 no. 14$_9$), is probably his elder son or perhaps, as Kirchner suggested (II^2 1941 ad loc.), his first cousin.

Λαφάης Σουνιεύς

PA 9004. Thesmothetes in 100/99 (II² 2336_{160}). His son Stratonikos (PA 12955) was an ephebe in 119/8 (II² $1008_{110\ IV}$).

[Λ]εώσ[τρα]τ̣ος Φιλοκράτου Φυλάσιος

PA 14631. This man was Priest of Roma(?) in 99/8 or 98/7 (II² 2336_{227}). Eubios (PA 5309), attested in a list of epimeletai of ca. 125 (II² 1939_{22}), was perhaps his older brother.

[Λυσίμαχος 'Αριστείδου] 'Ε̣[στιαι]όθεν

PA 9515. ἐπὶ τὴν φυλακὴν τῶν ἱερῶν χρημάτων in 97/6 (II² 2336_{233}, ID $1878b_{4}$); ἐπιμελητὴς ἐμπορίου in 94/3(?) (ID 2616_{3}). His wife 'Αμεινώ, son 'Αριστείδης, and daughter Νικοστράτη appear with him on ID 2616. The 'Α.Λ.'Ε. attested in a list of prominent men ca. 120 (II² 2452_{51}) was either his father or first cousin. The gravestone of the latter has survived (II² 6137/8).

Μαρσύας Μαρσύο[υ Με]λιτεύς

PA 9680. Priest of Artemis on the Island in 97/6 (II² 2336_{244}).

Μειδίας

PA 9716. Thesmothetes in 103/2 (II² 2336_{15}).

Μένανδρος Παιανιεύς

PA 9882. Thesmothetes in 100/99 (II^2 2336$_{157}$).

Μήδειος Μηδείου Πειραιεύς

PA 10098 and stemma. Child pythaïst in 128/7 (FD III 2 no. 12$_{4\ II}$), δηλιαστής in ca. 115 or perhaps a little earlier (ID 1869b), knight in the Pythaïs of 106/5 (FD III 2 no. 28$_{51\ IV}$), trierarch on Delos probably about the same time (ID 1841), Archon in 101/0 (II^2 2336$_{94}$, II^2 1028), Director of the Public Bank on Delos in 100/99 (II^2 2336$_{185}$ and supra p. 94 n. 14), Hoplite General in 99/8 (II^2 2336$_{165}$), Agonothetes of the Panathenaia in 99/8 (II^2 2336$_{183}$), Epimeletes of Delos in 98/7 (II^2 2336$_{189}$, ID 1757, 1711), Agonothetes of the Delia in 98/7 (II^2 2336$_{187}$), Archon from 91/0 to 89/8 (II^2 1713$_{9-11}$). He is also attested as Priest of Poseidon-Erechtheus ([Plut.] Decem Orat. Vitae 843 B), in a list of distinguished persons in ca. 120 (II^2 2452$_{29}$), and as an officer of prytaneis in ca. 100 B.C. (Agora XV 257$_{8-12}$ with Hesperia Suppl. 15 p. 84). His father, Medeios son of Lysander (PA 10097), served as exegete of the Eumolpidae ([Plut.] Decem Orat. Vitae 843 B). His son, Medeios (PA 10099), was pompostolos on Delos in ca. 100 (ID 2607$_5$), served as a mint magistrate with Diokles of Melite (Thompson, NSSCA p. 561) probably ca. 70 or even later, as Archon in ca. 65 (II^2 1340$_1$, II^2 2874, II^2 1095), and as exegete of the Eumolpidae in ca. 60 (II^2 3490). See ID 1869 for the female members of this family.

Μητρόδωρ[ος] (Μενεκλείδου) [Κυ]δαθηνα[ιεύς]

PA 10149 (stemma under PA 9902). Gymnasiarch on Delos in 103/2 (II^2 2336$_{29}$, ID 1927). His father, Menekleides (PA 9902), and brother Theophemos (PA 7097), are listed in II^2 2452, lines 48 and 59 with the name Ἱεροφάντης (see further Clinton, Trans. Am. Philosoph. Soc. 64, 1974, p. 28). The family thus belonged to the Eumolpidai and was active in the celebration of the Eleusinian Mysteries. A descendant is known as Kosmetes of ephebes in 13/2 (II^2 1963$_{3-4}$).

Μύρων Λευκονοεύς

PA 10505. Herald εἰς Δῆλον in 101/0 (II^2 2336$_{120}$). He is perhaps to be identified with Myron son of Philetairos who participated in the dramatic contests at Delphi in 106/5 (FD III 2 no. 49$_{30}$).

Ναυ[σί]στρατος Ἐροιά[δης]

Thesmothetes in 99/8 (II^2 2336$_{175}$).

Νικ[ίας]

Thesmothetes in 103/2 (II^2 2336$_{14}$).

Νικόνομ[ος _ca.7_ ἐκ] Κηδῶν

PA 10980. Thesmothetes in 97/6 (II^2 2336$_{251}$). Lewis (p. 288) identifies him with the third mint magistrate of ca. 109.

Νυμφόδωρος ἐκ Κεραμέων

PA 11147. Priest of Anios in 101/0 (II^2 2336_{129}).

Ξενοκλῆς Ῥαμνούσιος

PA 11231. ἐπὶ τὴν φυλακὴν τῶν ἱερῶν χρημάτων in 103/2 (II^2 2336_{35}); Thesmothetes in 100/99 (II^2 2336_{159}). A lineal descendant, Xenokles son of Theopompos of Rhamnous, was honored towards the end of the first century B.C. for overseeing the grain supply and having served as Hoplite General four times (II^2 3504).

[Ξε]νότιμος ἐγ Μυρρι[νο]ύττης

Proposer of the legislation which mandated II^2 2336 (II^2 2336_4).

Πανταкλῆς Βερενικίδης

PA 11591. Thesmothetes in 102/1 (II^2 2336_{60}).

Πολύκλειτο[ς Ἀλεξάνδρου Φλυ]εύς

PA 11978; stemmata in NPA p. 10 and in Roussel, DCA p. 111. Child pythaïst in 128/7 (FD III 2 no. $12_{4\ III}$); knight in 106/5 (Ibid. no. $28_{40\ I}$); Epimeletes of Delos in 99/8 (II^2 2336_{202}, ID 1619, 1709). His sons, Ἀλέξανδρος and Νικαγόρας, appear to have been child pythaïsts both in 106/5 and 98/7 (FD III 2 no. $15_{8\text{-}9\ III}$; nos. 31 and $17_{48\text{-}49}$ = Hesperia Suppl. 15 p. 54). The former rose to become Epimeletes of Delos in 54/3 (ID 1662). It seems more probable that the homonymous Archon of II^2 2870 is his grandson (as Kirchner in PA and Roussel, DCA p. 111) rather than the present man (as P. Graindor, Chronologie des archontes Athéniens p. 39) who would have been only in his early to middle 30's in 110/09.

Πόπλιος 'Αλαιεύς

PA 12114. Thesmothetes in 101/0 (II^2 2336_{102}).

Προκλῆ[ς _ _ _ _ _]

PA 12211. Archon in 99/8 (II^2 $2336_{163, 167, 239}$, ID 1619).

Π[ρωτ]ογένη[ς] (Λεωνίδου) [Φ]υλάδης

Priest of Sarapis in 106/5 (ID 2067, 2127, 2154); Priest of Apollo on Delos in 99/8 (II^2 2336_{240}).

Πυθίλαος [Σο]υνιεύς

PA 12359. Priest of Roma in 103/2 (II^2 2336_{40}). He is perhaps identical with Πυθίλας 'Απολλωνίου 'Ατταλίδος, ephebe in 128/7 (FD III 2 no. $24_{21\ I}$ and Hesperia 24, 1955, p. 232_{252}).

Πύθων (Φιλήμονος) Μελιτεύς

PA 12475 and 12467; NPA p. 148 and stemma on p. 163. Attested on Delos as a child celebrating the Hermaia ca. 125 (ID 2595_{31}); Nauarch in 102/1 (II^2 2336_{90}). His father is known from a Delian catalog of uncertain nature (ID 2630_{18}). His brother,

Philemon, is known as a child celebrating the Hermaia on Delos in ca. 125 (ID 2595_{17-18}) and as a knight in the Pythaïs of 106/5 (FD III 2 no. $28_{29\ II}$). His uncle, Python, appears as a hierope of the Romaia in 127/6 (ID 2596_{20}).

Πύρρος Πύρρου Λαμπτρεύς

PA 12520; stemma in Roussel, DCA p. 102. Participated as a knight in the Pythaïs of 128/7 (FD III 2 no. $27_{16\ I}$ and no. 38); third mint magistrate in 115/4 (Thompson, NSSCA p. 580; Mattingly, JHS 91, 1971 p. 91); Epimeletes of Delos in 104/3 (ID 2599); Director of the Public Bank on Delos in 99/8 probably (II^2 2336_{271}); Herald of the Council of the Areopagos in 98/7 (II^2 2336_{191}, FD III 2 nos. 10 and 2_{26} = Hesperia Suppl. 15 p. 50); Hoplite General in 97/6 (II^2 2336_{257}). Members of the family held prominent posts on Delos before him (see under Βύτταχος Πύρρου Λαμπτρεύς). A son Buttakos participated in the Pythaïs of 98/7 as a child pythaïst (FD III 2 nos. 31 and 17_{58} = Hesperia Suppl. 15 p. 54) and a daughter Anthe is attested as an ergastina in 108/7 (II^2 $1036_{32\ I}$ = BSA 21, 1914-16, p. 159).

[Σ]αραπίων (Σωτάδου) Αἰγ[ιλιεύς]

PA 12561; for a stemma see NPA p. 151. Priest of Anios in 102/1 (II^2 2336_{80}); Priest of Zeus Kynthios in 99/8 (ID 1886). His father (PA 13378) is known on Delos as Agoranomos ca. 150 (ID 1500_{27}, 1833) and as Paidotribes in 133/2 (ID 2594, 1946). The

Seleukos son of Sotades of Aigilia, pompostolos about the year 150 (ID 2609_{25}), is more probably his uncle than his brother (as NPA p. 151).

Σαραπίων Σαραπίωνος Μελιτεύς

PA 12564, NPA p. 149. Appears in a catalog of important men in ca. 120 (II^2 2452_{33}); participated as a knight in the Pythaïs of 106/5 (FD III 2 no. $28_{48\ IV}$); Hoplite General in 102/1 (II^2 2336_{51}); Epimeletes of Delos in 100/99 (II^2 2336_{141}, ID 2364); Hoplite General and leader of the Pythaïs in 98/7 (II^2 2336_{206}; FD III 2 no. 6_{5-7} = Hesperia Suppl. 15 p. 48; no. 16_2 = Hesperia Suppl. 15 p. 59). In this same period he was Agonothetes of the Eleusinia, Diasia, Panathenaia, and Delia (II^2 $2336_{207-214}$), was honored with a statue set up on the Acropolis (II^2 3881), and was commemorated on Delos as the patron of a man from Tyre (ID 2005). He had three daughters, Apollodora, Sosandra, and Theodora, and two sons, Diokles and Sarapion. Apollodora and Theodora were kanephoroi in the Pythaïs of 98/7 (FD III 2 nos. 31 and 17_{3-4} = Hesperia Suppl. 15 p. 54); Sosandra is attested as kanephoros at the Lenaia and ὑφιέρεια in the cult of Artemis on Delos (ID 1870); Diokles was kleidoukhos on Delos in 100/99 (ID 2364), pythaïst at Delphi in 98/7 (FD III 2 nos. 31 and 17_{16} = Hesperia Suppl. 15 p. 54), mint magistrate with Medeios' son in ca. 70 (Thompson, NSSCA p. 561), and perhaps brother-in-law to Medeios ([Plut.] Decem Orat. Vitae 843 B); Sarapion participated in the Pythaïs of 106/5 as a child pythaïst (FD III 2 no. $15_{11\ I}$) and in that of 98/7 as an ephebe (FD III 2 no. 26_{6} = Hesperia Suppl. 15 p. 57). Lineal descendants served as Hoplite General ([Plut.] Decem Orat. Vitae 843 B), as Archon (II^2 1343_{19-20}) and were active in the Genos of the Kerykes in ca. 20 B.C. (Trans. Am. Philosoph. Soc. 64, 1974, p. 51_{21-22}).

Σκαμά[ν]δρ[ιος Ὀλ]υμπίχου Ἀφιδναῖος

PA 12723. Thesmothetes in 98/7 (II^2 2336_{196}, FD III 2 nos. 10 and 2_{20} = Hesperia Suppl. 15 p. 50).

Σωσιγένης Ἐλαιούσιος

PA 13208. Polemarch in 100/99 (II^2 2336_{154}).

Σῶσος Φλυεύς

PA 13307. Thesmothetes in 100/99 (II^2 2336_{158}). His son or grandson served as a councillor in ca. 30 B.C. (Hesperia 47, 1978, p. 293_{34}).

Τιμόθεος Κ[ηφι]σιεύς

PA 13705. Thesmothetes in 100/99 (II^2 2336_{155}).

Τιμοῦχος (Τιμούχου) Ῥαμνούσι[ος]

PA 13830. General ἐπὶ τὴν παρασκευήν in 102/1 (II^2 2336_{89}). His brother, Lamios (PA 8986), was secretary in 112/1 (II^2 1012) and third mint magistrate twice at about the same period

(Lewis, p. 288). His nephew participated in the Pythaïs of 98/7 as a Dionysiac artist (FD III 2 no. 48_{31-32} = Hesperia Suppl. 15 p. 61).

Τίμων Σκαμ[β]ωνίδης

PA 13850. Priest of Anios in 103/2 (II^2 2336_{41}). A relative, perhaps his father, is Φαραδᾶς Τ. Σ. honored in a prytany inscription of ca. 150 B.C. (Agora XV 236_{42-45}).

Φιλέας 'Ε[φόρου] Πτελεάσιος

PA 14246. Thesmothetes in 98/7 (II^2 2336_{197}, FD III 2 nos. 10 and 2_{21} = Hesperia Suppl. 15 p. 50). His father, 'Ε. Νικάνορος Π., was Priest of Zeus Soter on Delos in 158/7 (ID 2605_{15}) and is known as a leaseholder in 156/5 (ID 1417B II_{147}).

Φιλήμων

PA 14269. ἐπὶ τὰ ἱερά in 101/0 (II^2 2336_{116}).

Φιλίων Φ[ιλίων]ος 'Ελευσίνιος

PA 14469. Secretary in 101/0 (II^2 1028_{1-2} = Hesperia Suppl. 15 p. 33); Thesmothetes in 98/7 (II^2 2336_{198}, FD III 2 nos. 10 and 2_{22} = Hesperia Suppl. 15 p. 50).

[Φ]ιλοκλῆς (Στασέου) [Κολωνῆθ]εν

PA 14550. Attested among youths celebrating the Hermaia in ca. 125 (ID 2595_9); he was Paidotribes with his father both on Delos in 104/3 (ID 2599_{10-11}) and in Athens in 97/6 (II^2 2990_{6-8}); Priest of Artemis on the Island in 101/0 (II^2 2336_{124}). His father, Staseas (PA 12875), was also Paidotribes on Delos in 133/2 (ID 2594 with 2589_{44}) and Priest of Sarapis in 118/7 (ID 2610_{25}, 2053, 2054).

Φιλομηλείδας Κυδαθη[να]ιεύς

PA 14656. Herald to Delos in 100/99 (II^2 2336_{143}).

Φίλων Παιανιεύς

PA 14861. Herald to Delos in 102/1 (II^2 2336_{91}).

Φυλότιμος Κικυννεύς

PA 15050. Thesmothetes in 101/0 (II^2 2336_{100}).
The [.....]σον Φυλοτίμου 'Αθηναῖον (Inschr. Perg. 268 C_7) who, dispatched by the proconsul Quintus Mucius Scaevola, arranged a treaty between the residents of Sardis and Ephesos in 94 B.C., is probably either the son or brother of the Thesmothetes.

[Χαρία]ς Χαρίου Αἰθαλίδης

PA 15335; stemma NPA p. 170. Listed among those celebrating the Hermaia on Delos ca. 125 (ID 2595_7); mint magistrate with his brother Dositheos in 99/8 (Mattingly, Historia 20, 1971, p. 36;

JHS 91, 1971, p. 91 with Badian, AJAH 1, 1976, pp. 117-118); στρατηγὸς ἐπὶ τὸ ναυτικόν in 98/7 (II^2 2336_{223}); ἐπὶ τὴν φυλακὴν τῶν ἱερῶν χρημάτων in 97/6 (II^2 2336_{234}, ID 1878). He is also known to have been Agoranomos (ID 2381) and paymaster of his prytany (Hesperia 36, 1967, p. 90_{60}). His father and uncle are attested on Delos in an inscription of ca. 150 (ID 2609_{22-23}); his brother Dositheos also appears on Delos among those celebrating the Hermaia in ca. 125 (ID 2595_{12}) and was an ephebe in Athens in 117/6 (II^2 $1009_{67\ II}$ with AJA 49, 1945, p. 435 n. 5).

[_ _ _ _]μόκριτος 'Αχαρ[νεύς]

PA II p. 524. ἐπὶ τὴν φυλακὴν τῶν ἱερῶν χρημάτων in 102/1 (II^2 2336_{70}).

[ca.5_]ος Εὐ[ω]νυμεύς

PA II p. 543. Thesmothetes in 101/0 (II^2 2336_{98}).

[ca.5_Εὐ]ωνυμεύς

PA II p. 543. Nauarch in 99/8 (II^2 2336_{166}).

[ca.4_]λης Θριάσιος

Thesmothetes in 99/8 (II^2 2336_{174}).

[ca.4]ιος ἐκ Κεραμέων

PA II p. 551. Agoranomos in 101/0 (II^2 2336_{113}). See epigraphical commentary.

[ca.6]ος Μαραθώνιος

PA II p. 578. Agoranomos on Delos in 102/1 (II^2 2336_{67}).

[ca.9 Ξ]υπεταιών

PA II p. 584. Agoranomos on Delos in 99/8 or 98/7 (II^2 2336_{225}).

[ca.8]νος ἐξ Οἴ[ο]υ

Priest of Apollo on Delos in 97/6 (II^2 2336_{231}). See epigraphical commentary.

[ca.11]ς Σουνιεύς

PA II p. 612 Basileus(?) in 102/1 (II^2 2336_{71}); See epigraphical commentary.

[ca.7]ίστρατος Σφήττιος

PA II p. 615. Herald of the Council of the Areopagos in 100/99 (II^2 2336_{151}).

[ca.3]ων Φλυεύ[ς]

Thesmothetes in 99/8 (II^2 2336_{172}).

[ca.4]κράτης Χολα[ργεύς]

Thesmothetes in 99/8 (II^2 2336_{173}).

INSCRIPTIONS CITED*

_FD_ III 2

---

*Inscriptional citations included in the prosopographical index are not separately indexed here.

ID

IG II^2

GENERAL INDEX

A

E

F

G

O

P

T

W

X

BIBLIOGRAPHY

Badian, E. "Rome, Athens, and Mithridates," AJAH 1 (1976) pp. 105-128.

Boethius, A. Die Pythaïs (Uppsala, 1918).

Bradeen, D.W. The Athenian Agora, XVII, Inscriptions: The Funerary Monuments (Princeton, 1974).

Bruneau, P. Recherches sur les cultes de Délos à l'époque hellénistique et à l'époque impérial, Bibl. Ec. fr. Ath. et Rome, fasc. 217 (Paris, 1970).

Busolt, G.-Swoboda, H. Griechische Staatskunde (Munich, 1926).

Clinton, K. "The Sacred Officials of the Eleusinian Mysteries," Trans. Am. Philosoph. Soc. 64 (1974).

Colin, G. Le culte d'Apollon pythien à Athènes (Paris, 1905).

_______. "Inscriptions de Delphes," BCH 30 (1906) pp. 161-329.

Couve, L. "Inscriptions de Delphès," BCH 18 (1894) pp. 70-100.

Daux, G. Delphes au IIe et Ier siècle (Paris, 1936).

Davies, J.K. Athenian Propertied Families (Oxford, 1971).

Day, J. An Economic History of Athens under Roman Domination (New York, 1942).

Deubner, L.A. Attische Feste (Berlin, 1932).

Dinsmoor, W.B. The Archons of Athens (Cambridge, 1931).

Dow, S. Conventions in Editing: GRBS Scholarly Aids 2 (Durham, 1969).

_____. "The Egyptian Cults in Athens," HThR 30 (1937) pp. 183-232.

_____. "The First Enneëteric Delian Pythaïs, IG II^2 2336," HSCP 51 (1940) pp. 111-124.

_____. "The Lists of Athenian Archontes," Hesperia 3 (1934) pp. 140-190.

Dow, S. "The List of Archontes, *IG* II^2 1706," *Hesperia* 2 (1933) pp. 418-446.

______. *Prytaneis*, *Hesperia* Suppl. 1 (Athens, 1937).

Eustratiadis, P. "Τὰ ἐκ τῆς Στήλης τῶν 'Απαρχῶν Τεμαχία," *'Επιγραφαὶ 'Ανέκδοτοι 'Ανακαλυφθεῖσαι καὶ 'Εκδοθεῖσαι ὑπὸ τοῦ 'Αρχαιολογικοῦ Συλλογοῦ* (Athens, 1855), fascicule 3, pp. 3-60.

Ferguson, W.S. *Athenian Tribal Cycles in the Hellenistic Age* (Cambridge, 1932).

______. *Hellenistic Athens* (London, 1911).

______. "The Oligarchic Revolution at Athens of the Year 103/2 B.C.," *Klio* 4 (1904) pp. 1-17.

______. "Researches in Athenian and Delian Documents I," *Klio* 7 (1907) pp. 213-240.

______. "Researches in Athenian and Delian Documents III," *Klio* 9 (1909) pp. 304-340.

Fouilles de Delphes, III, *Epigraphie*, ed. G. Colin et al. (Paris, 1909-1913).

Geagan, D.J. *The Athenian Constitution After Sulla*, *Hesperia* Suppl. 12 (Princeton, 1967).

Graindor, P. *Chronologie des archontes Athéniens sous l'Empire* (Brussels, 1922).

Gruen, E. "Rome and Rhodes in the Second Century B.C.," *CQ* 69 (1975) pp. 58-81.

Hansen, M.H. "Seven Hundred *Archai* in Classical Athens," *GRBS* 21 (1980) pp. 151-173.

Hatzfeld, J. *Les trafiquants italiens dans l'orient hellénique* (Paris, 1919).

Homolle, T. "Chronologie des archontes Athéniens," *BCH* 10 (1886) pp. 6-38.

______. "Les Romains à Délos," *BCH* 8 (1884) pp. 75-158.

Hutton, C.A. "The Greek Inscriptions at Petworth House," *BSA* 24 (1914-1916) pp. 155-163.

Die Inschriften von Pergamon, ed. M. Fraenkel (Berlin, 1890, 1895).

Inscriptiones Graecae, II-III, editio minor, ed. J. Kirchner (Berlin, 1913-1940).

Inscriptions de Délos, fascicule 3, ed. F. Dürrbach and P. Roussel (Paris, 1935); fascicules 4-5, ed. P. Roussel and M. Launey (Paris, 1937).

Kahrstedt, U. Untersuchungen zur Magistratur in Athen, II (Stuttgart, 1936).

Kirchner, J. Prosopographia Attica (Berlin, 1901, 1903).

Klaffenbach, G. Symbolae ad Historiam Collegiorum Artificum Bacchiorum (Berlin, 1914).

Koehler, U. Corpus Inscriptionum Atticarum, II (Berlin, 1883), no. 985.

Kourouniotis, K. Πρακτικά 1910 p. 142 no. 8.

Laidlaw, W.A. A History of Delos (Oxford, 1933).

Lewis, D.M. "The Chronology of the Athenian New Style Coinage," NC 7th Series 2 (1962) pp. 275-300.

MacKendrick, P. The Athenian Aristocracy 399-31 B.C. (Cambridge, 1969).

Mattingly, H.B. "Some Problems in Second Century Attic Prosopography," Historia 20 (1971) pp. 26-46.

____________. "Some Third Magistrates in the Athenian New Style Silver Coinage," JHS 91 (1971) pp. 85-93.

Mellor, R. ΘΕΑ ΡΩΜΗ, The Worship of the Goddess Roma in the Greek World, Hypomnemata 42 (Göttingen, 1975).

Meritt, B.D. and Traill, J.S. The Athenian Agora, XV, The Athenian Councillors (Princeton, 1974).

Mossé, C. Athens in Decline 404-86 B.C. (London, 1973).

Oliver, J. The Athenian Expounders of the Sacred and Ancestral Law (Baltimore, 1950).

Peek, W. "Attische Inschriften," Ath. Mitt. 67 (1942) pp. 1-217.

______. Kerameikos, Ergebnisse der Ausgrabungen, III, Inschriften, Ostraka, Fluchtafeln (Berlin, 1941).

Pickard-Cambridge, A.W. The Dramatic Festivals of Athens, 2nd ed. revised by J. Gould and D.M. Lewis (Oxford, 1968).

Pittakis, K.S. Ἐφημερὶς Ἀρχαιολογική, fascicule 39 (1854) nos. 2484, 2488, 2489, and 2493.

Reinmuth, O.W. "The Attic Archons Named Apolexis," BCH 90 (1966) pp. 93-100.

Rostovtzeff, M. The Social and Economic History of the Hellenistic World (Oxford, 1953).

Roussel, P. "Les Athéniens mentionnés dans les inscriptions de Délos," BCH 32 (1908) pp. 303-444.

_________. Les cultes égyptiens à Délos (Paris, 1916).

_________. Délos colonie athénienne (Paris, 1916).

Sarikakis, T. "οἱ Ἀθηναῖοι στρατηγοὶ τῶν Ἑλληνιστικῶν χρόνων," ΑΘΗΝΑ 57 (1953) pp. 242-304.

_________. "Αἱ ἐπὶ τοῦ ἐπισιτισμοῦ τῶν Ἀθηνῶν ἁρμοδιότητες τοῦ στρατηγοῦ ἐπὶ τὰ ὅπλα," Πλάτων 9 (1957) pp. 121-132.

_________. The Hoplite General in Athens, A Prosopography (Chicago, 1976).

von Schoeffer, V. De Deli Insulae Rebus (Berlin, 1889).

Sherk, R.K. Roman Documents from the Greek East (Baltimore, 1969).

Sifakis, G.M. Studies in the History of Hellenistic Drama (London, 1967).

Stanley, P.V. "Agoranomoi and Metronomoi: Athenian Market Officials and Regulations," Ancient World 2 (1979) pp. 13-18.

Stroud, R. "An Athenian Law on Silver Coinage," Hesperia 43 (1974) pp. 157-188.

Sundwall, J. Nachträge zur Prosopographia Attica (Helsingfors, 1910).

_________. Untersuchungen über die Attischen Münzen des Neueren Stils. Oefversigt of Finska Vetenskaps-Societens Forhändlar 45-50, 1906-1908 (Helsingfors, 1908).

Thompson, M. The New Style Silver Coinage of Athens (New York, 1961).

Tracy, S.V. "Athens in 100 B.C.," HSCP 83 (1979) pp. 213-235.

________. "Identifying Epigraphical Hands," GRBS 11 (1970) pp. 321-333.

________. The Lettering of an Athenian Mason, Hesperia Suppl. 15 (Princeton, 1975).

________. "Notes on the Inscriptions of the Pythaïs of 98/7," BCH 93 (1969) pp. 371-395.

________. "Notes on the Pythaïs Inscriptions," BCH 99 (1975) pp. 185-218.

Traill, J.S. The Political Organization of Attica, Hesperia Suppl. 14 (Princeton, 1975).

Travlos, J. Pictorial Dictionary of Ancient Athens (New York, 1971).

Wilhelm, A. "Attische Urkunden III," SAWW 202 5 abh. (1925) pp. 59-61.

________. "Vermuthungen," Philologus 60 (1901) pp. 481-490.

Wycherley, R.E. The Athenian Agora, III, The Literary and Epigraphical Testimonia (Princeton, 1957).

___________. "Two Athenian Shrines," AJA 63 (1959) pp. 68-72.

Hand A

'Αγαθῆ τύχη τῆς βουλῆς κ[αὶ το]ῦ δήμου τοῦ 'Αθηναίων· ὁ κεχειροτο<ν>[ημέν]ος ἐπὶ τὴν ἑξακοστο- NON-ΣΤΟΙΧ. ca. 68

vλὴν τῆς Πυθαΐδος καὶ τὰς ἀπαρχὰς τῆς πρώτης ἐν⟦νεετη⟧ρί[δος 'Αμφικρ]άτης 'Επιστράτου Πε-

3. ριθοίδης ἀνέγραψ[εν] τοὺς δόντας τῶν ἀρχόν[των τὰς ἀπαρ]χὰς [τ]ῶι 'Από[λλωνι] τῶι Πυθίωι κα-

vτὰ τὸ ψήφισμα [ὃ Ξε]νότιμος ἐγ Μυρρι[νο]ύττης εἶπεν. vacat (0.309 m.)

a. 103/2 a. 5. vvvvvοἵδε ἀπήρξαντο ἐπὶ Θεοκλέους ἄ[ρχον]τος

[στρα]τ[ηγ]ὸς ἐ[πὶ] τὰ ὅπλα ⟦v'Αμμώνιο⟧ς

[vv⟦Δημητρίο]υ 'Αναφλύστ⟧ιος ΗΗ

[κῆρυξ βουλῆς τ]ῆς ἐξ 'Αρείου πάγου

9. v'Η[_ _ _ _ _ _ _ _ _ _ _ _ _ _ Η]

ἄρχων [Θεοκλῆς _ _ _ _ _ _ _ _ _ Η]

βασιλεὺς [_ _ _ _ _ _ _ _ _ _ _ Η]

12. πολέμαρχ[ος _ _ _ _ _ _ _ _ _ _ Η]

[θεσ]μοθέτ[αι _ _ _ _ _ _ _ _ _ Η]

Νικ[ίας _ _ _ _ _ _ _ Η]

15. ⟦Μειδ⟧ίας [_ _ _ _ _ Η]

Δωσίθεος [_ _ _ _ _ _ Η]

Διονύσιος Χ[_ _ _ _ _ Η]

18. 'Απολλώνιος [_ _ _ _ _ Η]

ναύαρχος Κηφισ[_ _ _ _ _ _ _ _ ⚑]

στρατηγὸς ἐπὶ τ[ὴν παρασκευὴν]

21. vτὴν ἐν ἄστει 'Ιάσ[ων _ _ _ _ _ ⚑]

ἐπιμελητὴς τ[οῦ ἐμ Πειραιεῖ λιμέ]-

vνος Δημέας 'Α[λαιεὺς Η]

24. [ἐπιμελ]ητὴς [Δήλου]

[vΔιοσκουρίδης _ _ _ _ _ _ ΗΗ]

[ἐπιμελητὴς ἐμπορίου]

27. vΙ[_ _ _ _ _ _ _ _ _ _ ΗΗ]

γυμν[ασίαρχος εἰ]ς Δῆ[λον]

vΜητρόδωρ[ος Κυ]δαθηνα[ιεὺς Η]

30. ἀγορανόμοι [εἰ]ς Δῆλον

[vΚιχη]σίας Σουνιεὺς [Η]

'Ερμοκλῆς [ca.5]ο[_ _ _ Η]

33. ἐπὶ τὴν φυλακὴν τῶν ἱ[ερ]ῶν χρη-

vμάτων Θεότιμος Αἰξωνεὺς Η

Ξενοκλῆ⟦ς⟧ 'Ραμνούσιος Η

36. ἱερεὺς 'Απόλλωνος ἐν Δήλωι

v'Αμμώνιος <Π>αμβωτάδης Η

ἱερεὺς 'Αρτέμιδος ἐν νή⟦.⟧σωι

39. v'Αγαθοκλῆς v⟦'Αγκυλῆ⟧[θ]εν Η

ἱερεὺς 'Ρώμης Πυθίλαος [Σο]υνιεὺς Η

ἱερεὺς 'Α⟦νvίv⟧ου Τίμων Σκαμ[β]ωνίδης ⚑

42. ἱερεὺς Σαράπιδος ἐν Δή<λ>[ωι Δ]ράκων ⚑

ἱερεὺς ἁγνῆς θεοῦ Διόδ[ον]τος Μαρ⟦αθ⟧ώ⟦..⟧ Η

κῆρυξ εἰς Δῆλον Γλαυκία[ς Κρι]ωεὺς Η

45. ἱερεὺς Διὸς Κυνθίου Ζή[ν]ων [⟦Κ]ηφισιε⟧ὺς Η

ἱερεὺς Διονύσου vacat ⚑

vacat

Hand B

a. 102/1 a.

48. [οἵ]δε [ἀπέδωκαν τ]ὰς ἀπαρχὰς

[ἐπὶ 'Εχεκράτ]ους ἄρχοντος

[σ]τρατη[γὸς] ἐπὶ τὰ ὅπλα

51. Σαραπίω[ν Μ]ελιτεὺς ΗΗ

ἄρχων 'Εχεκράτη[ς Τρινεμ]εεὺς Η

vacat

54. πολέμαρχος ⟦Διότιμος.⟧ Μαραθώνιος Η

θεσμοθέται

'Αριστώνυμος 'Ελευσίνιος Η

57. Θέων 'Ερχιεὺς Η

Βάκχιος 'Αχαρνεὺς [Η]

['Α]λκιβιάδης vΠοτάμιος [Η]

60. Πανταχλῆς vΒερενικίδης Η

vacat (0.361 m.)

Hand D

150. [κῆρυξ β]ουλῆς τῆς ἐξ 'Αρείου πάγου

[_ ca.7_]ίστρατος Σφήττιος Η

[ἄρ]χω[ν Θε]οδόσ[ιο]ς Λακιάδης Η

153. [β]ασιλε[ὺ]ς Καλλίμαχος Λευκονοεὺς Η

[π]ολέμα[ρ]χος Σωσιγένης 'Ελαιούσιος Η

θεσμοθέ[ται] Τιμόθεος Κ[ηφι]σιεὺς Η

156. Δωσίθεος [ἐ]γ Μυρρινού[τ]της Η

Μένανδρος Παιανιεὺς Η

Σῶσος Φλυεὺς Η

159. Ξενοκλῆς 'Ραμνούσιος Η

Λαφά⟦ης.⟧ Σουνιεὺς Η

vacat

Hand B

a. 99/8 a.

162. οἵδε ἀπέδωκαν τὰς ἀπαρχὰς

ἐπὶ Προκλέου[ς ἄ]ρχοντος

vvvvστ[ρατηγὸς] ἐπὶ τὰ ὅπλα

Hand M

165. [Μήδειος Μηδείου] Πειραιεὺς ΗΗ

Hand X

[ναύαρχος ca.5_ Εὐ]ωνυμεὺς ⚑

Hand D

[ἄρχων Προκλῆς _ _ _ _] Η

168. [βασιλεὺς _ _ _ _ _ _ _ _ _ _] Η

[πολέμαρχος _ _ _ _ _ _ _ _ _ _] Η

[θεσμοθέται _ _ _ _ _ _ _ _ _ _] Η

171. [_ca.6 _]ΣΟ[_ _ _ _ _] Η

[ca.3]ων vΦλυεὺ[ς Η]

[ca.4]κράτης Χολα[ργεὺς Η]

174. [ca.4]λης Θριάσιος [Η]

Ναυ[σί]στρατος 'Ερχιά[δης Η]

ἐμπ[ο]ρίου ἐπιμελητὴς

Hand E

177. v'Αρχίας Διογένου 'Ανα[φλύστιος ΗΗ]

Hand B

στρατηγὸς ἐπὶ τ[ὴν παρασκευὴν]

Διονύσιος Δημη[τρίου Αἰξ]ων[εὺς ⚑]

Hand E

180. ⟦κῆρυξ βουλῆς τῆς ἐξ 'Αρείο[υ πά]γο⟧υ

Η vv'Αθηνόδωρος 'Αθηνογένου Α[ἰξ]ωνεὺς [Η]

Hand M

<ἀ>γωνοθέτης Παναθηναίων

Η 183. vv⟦Μήδειος⟧ Μηδείου Πειραιεὺς ΗΗ⚑

ἐπὶ τὴν δημοσίαν τράπεζαν τὴν ἐν Δήλωι

vv⟦Μήδειο[ς⟧ Μ]ηδείου Πειραιεὺς ΗΗ

186. ἀγωνοθέτ[ης Δ]ηλίων

vv⟦Μήδειος⟧ [Μηδείο]υ Πειραιεὺς ΗΗ⚑

ἐπιμελητὴ[ς Δήλου]

189. vv⟦Μήδειος⟧ Μηδ[είου ⟦....].....⟧ ΗΗ

Hand N

κῆρυξ βουλῆς τῆς ἐξ 'Αρε[ίου π]άγου

vΠύρρος Πύρρ<ο>υ Λαμπ⟦τρε⟧ὺ[ς] [Η]

192. ἄρχων 'Αργεῖος 'Αργεί⟦ου Τρικορύσιο⟧ς [Η]

βασιλεὺς 'Αρχωνίδης Ναυκράτου ἐκ Κεραμέω[ν Η]

πολέμαρχος 'Αριστίων Εὐδόξου Μελιτεὺς Η

195. θ[εσμοθ]έται 'Απο[λλ]ώνιος Νικάνδρου Κυθήρριος Η

[θ]εόπομπος Κεφ[αλῆθ]ε[ν] Η
vacat
63. vacat
[ἐπιμελητὴς Δήλου Θεόδο]τος Σουνιεὺς ΗΗ
[ἐπιμελητὴς ἐμπορίου] ἐν Δήλωι
66. [_ _ _ca.16_ _ _]ς ΗΗ
[ἀγορανόμοι _ca.6]ος Μαραθώνιος
[_ _ _ca.16_ _ _]ος ΗΗ
69. [ἐπὶ τὴν φυλακὴν τῶν ἱε]ρῶν χρημά[των]
[_ _ _ca.20_ _ _ _ _ _ _]μόκριτος Ἀχαρ[νεὺ]ς ΗΗ
[_ _ _ca.20_ _ _ _ _ _ _]ς Σουνιεὺς Η
72. [_ _ _ _ca.20_ _ _ _ _ _ _]ειος Η
[γυμνασίαρχος εἰς τὸ ἐν Δήλωι γ]υμνάσιον
[_ _less than ca.22_ _ _] Η
75. [ἱερεὺς Ἀπόλλωνος ἐν Δήλωι]
[ca.7_ _]ίων vv[_ _ _ _ Η]
[ὁ ἐπὶ τὴ]ν τράπεζ[αν τὴν ἐν Δήλωι]
78. Καλλί[ας] vv Ἀθμον[εὺς ΗΗ]
ἱερεὺς Διο[νύ]σου Θεόδοτ[ος _ _ _ _ 𐅅]
ἱερεὺς Ἀνίο[υ Σ]αραπίων Αἰγ[ιλιεὺς 𐅅]
81. ἱερεὺς Ἀρτέμ[ιδο]ς ἐν νήσ<ω>[ι]
Θεόμνηστος [Κυδα]θηναιεὺ[ς Η]
ἱερεὺς Σαράπιδος Α[ca.4]ης Θορίκ[ιος 𐅅]
84. ἱερεὺς ἁγνῆς θεοῦ Θεα[_ca.6] Ἀγγ[ελῆθεν Η]
ἱερεὺς Διὸς Κυνθίου Δημήτ[ριος _ _ _ _ Η]
ἐπιμελητὴς τοῦ ἐμ Πειρα[ιεῖ λιμένος]
87. Βύτταπος v Λαμπτρε[ὺς Η]
στρατηγὸ<ς> ἐπὶ [τ]ὴν παρασ[κευὴ]ν τὴν ἐν ἄστει
Τιμοῦχος v Ῥαμνούσι[ος] 𐅅
90. ναύαρχος Πύθων v Μελιτεὺς 𐅅
Hand X κῆρυξ εἰς Δῆλον Φίλων Παιανιεὺς Η
Hand C οἵδε ἀπέδωκαν τὰς ἀπαρχὰς ἐπὶ Μηδείου
a. 101/0 a. 93. στρατηγὸς ἐπὶ τὰ ὅπλα Ἀπο[λλό]δωρος Δ[_ca.7 ΗΗ]
[ἄρ]χων Μήδ[ειος Πειραιεὺς Η]
[βασιλεὺς Ἡ]ρόδοτ[ο]ς Προβα[λίσιος Η]
96. [πολέμαρχ]ος Ἀντίπατρος Κυδα[θηναιεὺς Η]
θεσμοθέται
[ca.5]ος Εὐ[ω]νυμεὺς [Η]
99. Ἀρτεμίδωρος Βερενικίδης [Η]
Φυλότιμος Κικυννεὺς [Η]
Ἀ[[π]]ολλωνίδης Λακιάδ[η]ς [Η]
102. Πόπλιος Ἀλαιεὺς Η
Hand X κῆρυξ Ἀρεοπαγιτῶν Θεόχαρις ἐκ Κεραμέων Η
Hand C στρατηγὸς ἐπὶ τὴν παρασκευὴν
105. Διονυσογένης Ἀνα[γ]υράσιος <Ρ>
ἐπιμελ<η>τὴς Πε[ιραιέ]ως
Κηφισόδωρος Αἰ[ξων]εὺς Η
108. ἐπιμελητὴς Δή[λου]
Καλλίστρατ[ος ca.4]εὺς ΗΗ
ἐπιμελητὴ[ς ἐμ]πορίο[υ]
111. Ἀριστίων v[ἐ]ξ Οἴου ΗΗ
ἀγορανόμοι
[ca.4]ιος ἐκ Κερα[[μέω]]ν, Ἀλέξανδρος ΗΗ
114. ἐπὶ τ<ὰ> ἱερὰ
Δεινίας Παλληνεὺς Η
Φιλήμων Η

Σκαμά[ν]δρ[ιος Ὀλ]υμπίχου Ἀφιδναῖος Η
Φιλέας Ἐ[φόρου] Πτελεάσιος Η
198. Φιλίων Φ[ιλίων]ος Ἐλευσίνιος Η
Βούλων Λ[εωστ]ράτου Παλληνεὺς Η
Λακρατείδη[ς Σωστ]ράτου Ἰκαριεὺς Η
201. ἐπιμελητὴ[ς Δήλου] Hand X
v[[Πολύκλειτο[ς]? Ἀλεξάνδρου Φλυ]εὺς ΗΗ
vἐπὶ τὰ ἱερὰ Θεό[χαρις Ἑστιαίου ἐκ Κερα]μέων Η Hand E
204. οἵδε ἀπέδωκ[αν τὰς ἀπαρχὰς ἐπὶ] Ἀργείου ἄρχοντος a. 98/7 a.
vvστρατηγὸς [ἐπὶ τὰ ὅπλα]
[Σ]αραπίων Σαρα[πίωνος Μελιτ]εὺς ΗΗ
207. [vvἀ]γωνοθέτης Ἐλ[ευσινίων]
Σαραπίων Σαραπ[ίωνος Μελιτεὺς] ΗΗ𐅅
vvἀγων[οθέτ]ης Δια[σίων]
210. Σαραπίων [Σαρα]πί[ωνος Μελιτεὺς] ΗΗ[[.]]
vvἀγωνοθέτη[ς] Πα[ναθηναίων]
[Σαρ]απίων Σαραπ[ίωνος Μελιτεὺς ΗΗ]𐅅
213. [vvἀγ]ωνοθέτης Δηλί[ων]
[Σαραπί]ων Σαραπί[ωνος Μελιτεὺς ΗΗ𐅅]
[vvστρατηγὸ]ς ἐπ[ὶ τὴν παρασκευὴν]
216. [_ ca.9 _]ς Διο[_ _ _ _ _ _ _ 𐅅]
[vἐπὶ τὰ ἱερὰ] Διοφά[ντος Ἀριστοκλέους Μαραθώνιος Η] Hand X
ἱερεὺς ἁγνῆ[ς] Ἀφροδ[ίτης ἐν Δήλωι] Hand H
219. Θεόβιο[ς] Διον[υ]σίου Ἀ[χαρνεὺς Ρ]
[ἐπιμελ]ητ[ὴς] Πειραι[έως] Hand X
[ca.5]ω[1-2]θεος Χ[_ _ _ _ _ _ Η]
222. [στρατηγ]ὸς ἐπὶ τὸ ναυ[τικὸν]
[vΧαρία]ς Χαρίου Αἰθαλίδης [𐅅]
[ἐπὶ _7-8_] ἄρχοντος ἀγορανόμος εἰς Δῆλον Hand X
225. [_ ca.9 _ Ξ]υπεταιὼν Η
[_ ca.10 _ Δη]μ[ήτ]ριος Θεοδοσίου Λακιάδης Η Hand D
[_ ca.10 _ Λ]εώσ[τρα]τος Φιλοκράτου Φυλάσιος Η
228. [vvἐπιμε]λητὴ[ς] Δήλου [[..]] Hand G
[Ἀριστίων] Σωκράτου ἐ[ξ Οἴ]ου ΗΗ
[vvἱερεὺ]ς Ἀπόλλων[ο]ς ἐν Δήλωι [[.]]
231. [_ ca.8 _]νος ἐξ Οἴ[ο]υ Η
[vἐπὶ τὴν φυλακὴν] τῶν [ἱε]ρῶν χρημάτων
[Λυσίμαχος Ἀριστείδου] Ἑ[στιαι]όθεν Η
234. [Χαρίας Χαρίου] Αἰθαλίδη[ς] Η
[vvἐπιμελ]ητὴς Πε[ιραιέ]ως
[[_ ca.9 _]][_ca.7_]ης Η
237. ἱερεὺ[ς ἁγνῆς Ἀφροδίτη]ς ἐν Δήλωι Hand B
vvΓάι[ος Γαίου Ἀχαρνεὺ]ς Η
ἐπὶ Προκλ[έους ἄρχοντος ἱερε]ὺς Ἀπόλλωνος Hand X
240. ἐν Δήλωι Π[ρωτ]ογένη[ς Φ]ιλάδης Η
ἱερεὺς Διὸς Κυν[θίου ἐ]ν Δήλῳ Hand H
Θεόβιος Διονυσ[ίου] Ἀχαρνεὺς Ν
243. ἱερεὺς Ἀρτέμι[δο]ς ἐν νήσωι Hand B

117. γυμνασίαρχος εἰς {ις} Δῆ[λ]ον
Διονυσόδωρος Δειρ[αδιώτη]ς H
κῆρυξ εἰς Δῆλον
120. Μύρων Λευκονοεὺς H
ἱερεὺς Ἀπόλλωνος ἐν Δήλωι
Ἀντικράτης Ἐπικηφίσιος [H]
Hand B 123. ἱερεὺς Ἀρτέμιδος [ἐ]ν νήσωι
[Φ]ιλοκλῆς [Κολωνῆθ]εν H
[ἱερ]εὺς Διο[νύσου]
126. Ἀσκληπιά[δης Ἁλαι]εὺς 𐅄
Hand X ἱερεὺς Ῥώμης
Δημ<ή>τρι<ο>ς Αἰ<ξ>ω[νεὺ]ς H
Hand X 129. ἱερεὺς Ἀνίου Νυμφόδωρος 𐅄
[[ᵛἐ κ Κ ε ρ α μ έ ω ν]]
Hand E ἱερεὺς ἁγνῆς θεοῦ ἐν Δήλωι
132. Ἀριστόνους Πρωτάρχου Σφήττιος [H]
Hand H ἱερεὺς Σαράπιδος ἐν Δήλ[ωι]
Θεόβιος Διονυσίου Ἀχ[[αρνεὺ]]ς N
135. vacat
Hand X οἵδε ἀπέδωκαν τὰς ἀπαρχὰς
a. 100/99 a. ἐπὶ Θεοδοσίου ἄρχοντο[ς]
Hand E 138. στρατηγὸς ἐπὶ τ[ὰ ὅπλα]
Ἑστιαῖος [Θε]οχάριδος ἐκ Κεραμέων HH
Hand X ἐπιμελητὴς Δήλου
141. Σαρ[α]πίων Μελιτεὺς HH
Hand D κῆρυξ εἰς Δῆλον
Φιλομηλείδας Κυδαθη[να]ιεὺς H
Hand X 144. ἐπιμελητὴς τοῦ ἐν Πειραιεῖ
λιμένος Διονύσιος Παλληνεὺς H
Hand E ναύαρχος Θέων Παιονίδης 𐅄
Hand B 147. ἱερεὺς Ἀπόλλων[ος] ἐν Δήλωι
Δημήτριος Δημ[ητρίου]ου
Ἀ[[ν]]αφλύσ[τιος H]
vacat (0.028 m.)

Μαρσύας Μαρσύο[υ Με]λιτεὺς [H]
κῆρυξ βουλῆς τῆς ἐξ [Ἀρεί]ου πάγου Hand F
246. Ἀνδρέας Ἀνδρέου [Πειραιεὺς] H
[ἄρ]χων Ἡ[ρ]άκλειτος Ἡρ[_ ca.7 _] Σφήττιος H
βα[σιλεὺς] Ἀρίστων Π[αντακ]λέους Γαργήττιος H
249. πολ[έμαρχ]ος Ἀντικράτ[ης Φιλίσκο]υ Ἐπικηφίσιος H
[θεσμ]οθ[έται]
Νικόνομ[ος _ ca.7 _ ἐκ] Κηδῶν H
252. Διογένης [ca.4 Κυδαθ]ηναιεὺς H
Δημήτριος Δ[ca.6 Παι]ονί[δη]ς H
Κλειτόμαχος [_ ca.7 _] Φλυεὺς H
255. Ζήνων Ἀρίσ[τωνος Μ]αραθώνιος H
Ἀργεῖος Ἀ[σκλαπίωνος Ἀτ]ηνεὺς H
στρατηγὸς ἐπὶ [τὰ ὅπλ]α Πύρρος Πύρρου Λαμπτρεὺς HH Hand B
258. ᵛστρατηγὸς ἐπὶ τὸ ναυτικὸν Hand X
Ἀρχίας Διογένου [Ἀνα]φλύστιος 𐅄
ἱερεὺςᵛΣαράπ[ιδος ἐν] Δήλωι Hand X
261. ᵛᵛᵛΕὐκ[τ]ύμε[νος Εὐδή]μου Εἰτεαῖος 𐅄
στρατηγὸς [ἐπὶ τὴν πα]ρασκευὴν τὴν ἐν ἄστει Hand B
Ἀγαθοκλῆς Σω[σ]ικρά[το]υ Οἰναῖος 𐅄
264. ἱερεὺς Ῥώμης Hand X
Δημήτριος Ἀσκληπίδου Ἁλαιεὺς H
ᵛᵛστρατηγὸ[ς] ἐπὶ τὸ ναυτικὸν Hand O
267. ᵛἈρχ[ίας] Ἀρχεστράτου Κυδαθηναιεὺς 𐅄
γυμνα[σίαρ]χος εἰς τὸ ἐν Δήλωι γυμνάσιον
Δάμων [Ἰκ]αριεὺς H
270. [[ὁ]] ἐπὶ τὴν δ[η]μοσίαν τράπεζαν τὴν [[3½]] Hand B
[ἐν] Δήλωι Πύ[ρρ]ος Πύρρου Λαμπτρεὺς HH
vacat (0.062 m.)

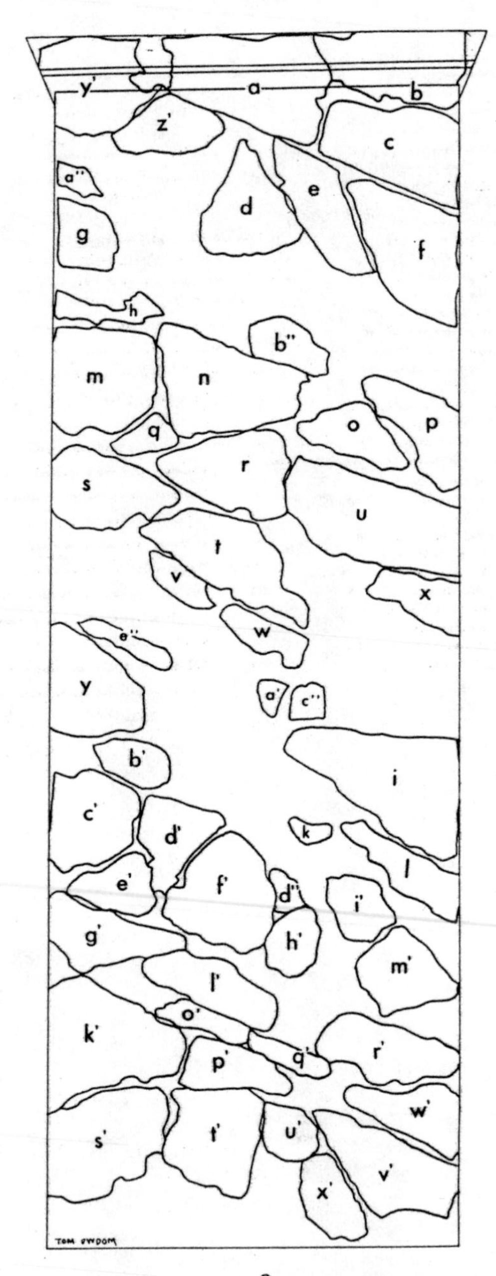

Fig. I. Drawing of IG II^{2} 2336 by T. Owdonn.

Fig. 2. IG II[2] 2336 (top).

Fig. 3. IG II^2 2336 (middle).

Fig. 4 IG II^{2} 2336 (bottom).

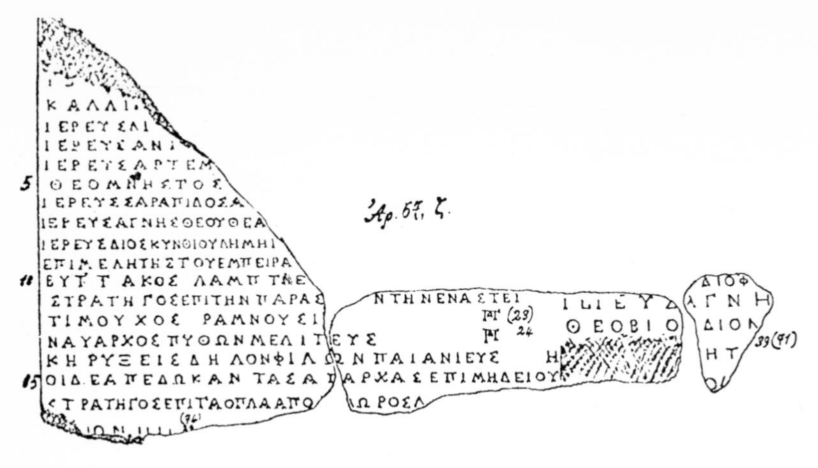

Fig. 5. Frgs. y, z, a' (after Eustratiadis); lines 78 - 94, 217 - 221.

Fig. 6. Frgs. n', m' (after Eustratiadis); lines 247 - 253.

Fig. 7. Agora I 3318, frg. g'' (courtesy of Athenian Agora Excavations); lines 246 - 248.

Fig. 8. Agora I 4037, frg. h'' (courtesy of Athenian Agora Excavations); lines 180 - 182.

Fig. 9. Agora I 5044, frg. f'' (courtesy of Athenian Agora Excavations); lines 227 - 233.

Fig. 10. Hand A, lines 28 - 43.

Fig. 11. Hand B, lines 78 - 91.

Fig. 12. Hand C, lines 114 - 122.

Fig. 13. Hand D, lines 154 - 160.

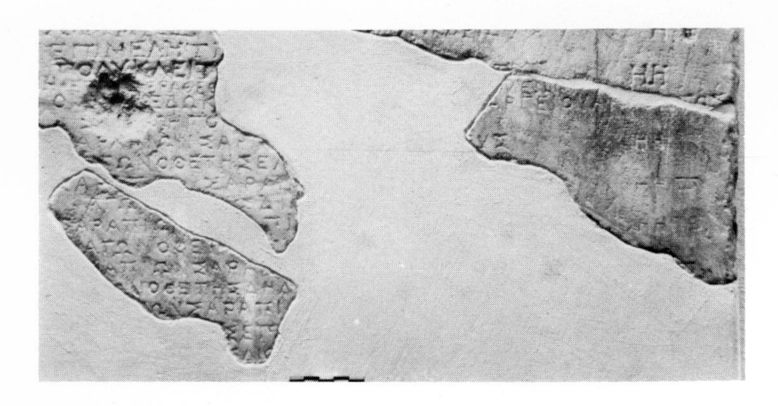

Fig. 14. Hand E, lines 201 - 216.

Fig. 15. Hand F, lines 244 - 257.

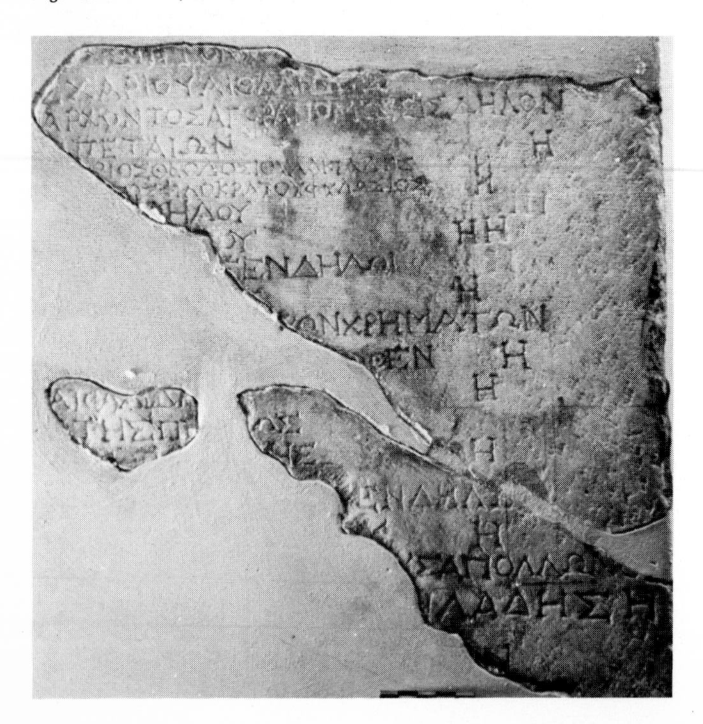

Fig. 16. Hand G, lines 222 - 242.

Fig. 17. Hand H, lines 125 - 138.

Fig. 18. Hand M, lines 182 - 190.

Fig. 19. Hand N, lines 193 - 201.

Fig. 20. Hand O, lines 265 - 269.

Fig. 22. Lines 126 - 149.

Fig. 21. Lines 94 - 99.

Fig. 24. Agora I 7361, frg. i'' (copyright by Agora Excavations, 1982); lines 268 - 271.

Fig. 23. Lines 257 - 271.